Strictly Come Dancing

PUZZLE
BOOK

THE OFFICIAL

Strictly Come Dancing

PUZZLE BOOK

NEIL SOMERVILLE

BBC BOOKS

BBC Books, an imprint of Ebury Publishing

UK | USA | Canada | Ireland | Australia
India | New Zealand | South Africa

BBC Books is part of the Penguin Random House group of companies
whose addresses can be found at global.penguinrandomhouse.com

Penguin Random House UK
One Embassy Gardens, 8 Viaduct Gardens, London SW11 7BW

penguin.co.uk
global.penguinrandomhouse.com

Penguin Random House UK

First published by BBC Books in 2025

1

Text by Neil Somerville
Cover design by Toby Clarke
The moral right of the author has been asserted.

This book is published to accompany the television series Strictly Come Dancing,
first broadcast on BBC One in 2004. This series (Series 23) first broadcast 2025.

Executive Producer: Sarah James
Series Director: Nikki Parsons
Series Editors: Jack Gledhill and Nicola Fitzgerald
BBC Studios Brand Marketing Team: Rose Sammut, Harriet Frost
and Charlotte Edwards

Designed and set by seagulls.net

Printed and bound in Great Britain by Clays Ltd, Elcograf S.p.A.

The authorised representative in the EEA is Penguin Random House Ireland,
Morrison Chambers, 32 Nassau Street, Dublin D02 YH68.

A CIP catalogue record for this book is available from the British Library

ISBN 9781785949463

Project Editors: Katie Fisher, Clementine Lussiana

MIX
Paper | Supporting responsible forestry
FSC® C018179
FSC www.fsc.org

Penguin Random House is committed to a sustainable future for our business, our readers and our planet. This book is made from Forest Stewardship Council® certified paper.

Strictly fans are special people and their devotion and dedication to the show is fantastic.

Craig Revel Horwood

As a *Strictly* fan
this book is dedicated to you.

Every year the celebrities on *Strictly* take on the challenge of not only learning to dance but to dance to exacting standards. In the process we share in their journey, seeing successes as well as disappointments. *Strictly* is a magical journey – an exciting one full of surprise, drama and sparkle.

Over the years this award-winning series has created many special moments and, whenever it is on, continues to enthral.

This puzzle book helps celebrate the joy, fun and rich history of *Strictly* with a mix of puzzles to tackle and enjoy. Whether solving mystery sudokus, deliberating over what judges and celebrities may have said, or testing your *Strictly* knowledge, there is plenty to delight and ponder over. Some may even lead you on a merry dance!

Have fun, enjoy the puzzles and immerse yourself in the magic that is *Strictly*.

Neil Somerville

You can find all the answers to the puzzles that follow on pages 216–231. Good luck!

~ 1 ~

ANAGRAMS

Unscramble the following to reveal dances seen on *Strictly.*

1. A bold pose
2. Choral nest
3. Not engage in art
4. Ah, some romantic
5. Zeal wins event

~ 2 ~

CROSS OUT

Cross out all the letters that appear more than once. The remaining letters, reading from top to bottom and left to right, will spell out something often seen and enjoyed on *Strictly*. What is it?

C	M	A	H	F	P	N	G
R	L	O	D	Q	K	B	T
G	U	Y	S	W	R	X	Z
B	P	K	T	M	D	H	O
W	Z	J	C	Q	X	I	U
L	V	S	Y	E	A	N	F

~ 3 ~

MYSTERY SUDOKU

Complete the grid so that every row, column and 3 × 3 box contains the letters ELMOPRSTU in any order. One row or column contains a seven-letter word – something that is important for dancers to get right. What is it?

P					E	M	S	R
				M			E	U
			U		P			T
			L					
	E	O				R	T	
					T			
E			T		U			
M	S			L				
L	R	T	P					S

~ *4* ~

TRIVIA

1. In which year did *Strictly Come Dancing* begin?
2. How many couples were in the first series?
3. The second series featured the first celebrity to receive a perfect 40. Who was it?
4. What did Len Goodman say he was going to pickle?
5. Which dance was introduced into the competition in 2009?
6. Dr Punam Krishan created *Strictly* history in series 22's Movie Week by performing what sort of dance?
7. In which dance would you most likely see a fleckerl?

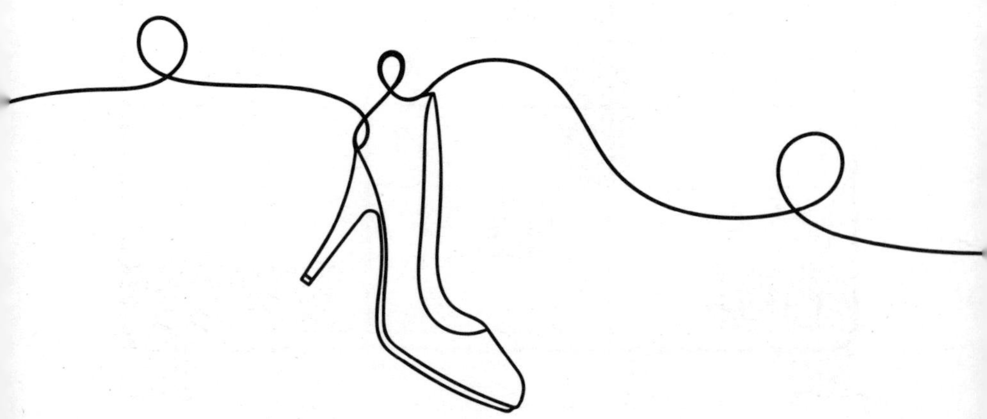

~ 5 ~

LETTER DROP

The letters in each of the columns need to be entered into the squares directly below, but not necessarily in the same order. By placing the letters in the correct squares, you will discover Craig Revel Horwood's amusing observation after watching Jake Wood's salsa.

		U			N	U			
	I	A		O	C	O	T		
Y	C	C	T	H	C	T	U	O	N
H	O	P	R	A	A	K	I	S	D
T	H	O	C	A	C	V	E	L	A
			■					■	
			■						
				■					
■	■						■	■	■
■									■

~6~

CRISS-CROSS

All the following celebrities have graced the *Strictly* dance floor. Can you find a place for each in the grid?

6 LETTER NAME

JB Gill

7 LETTER NAMES

Sam Quek

Tom Dean

8 LETTER NAMES

James Bye

Kym Marsh

Matt Goss

9 LETTER NAMES

Pete Wicks

Tony Adams

10 LETTER NAMES

Adam Thomas

Jamie Laing

John Whaite

Paul Merson

Sara Davies

Shayne Ward

Will Mellor

Wynne Evans

11 LETTER NAMES

Hamza Yassin

Nick Knowles

Nikita Kanda

Tasha Ghouri

12 LETTER NAMES

Annabel Croft

Toyah Willcox

13 LETTER NAME

Angela Scanlon

14 LETTER NAME

Layton Williams

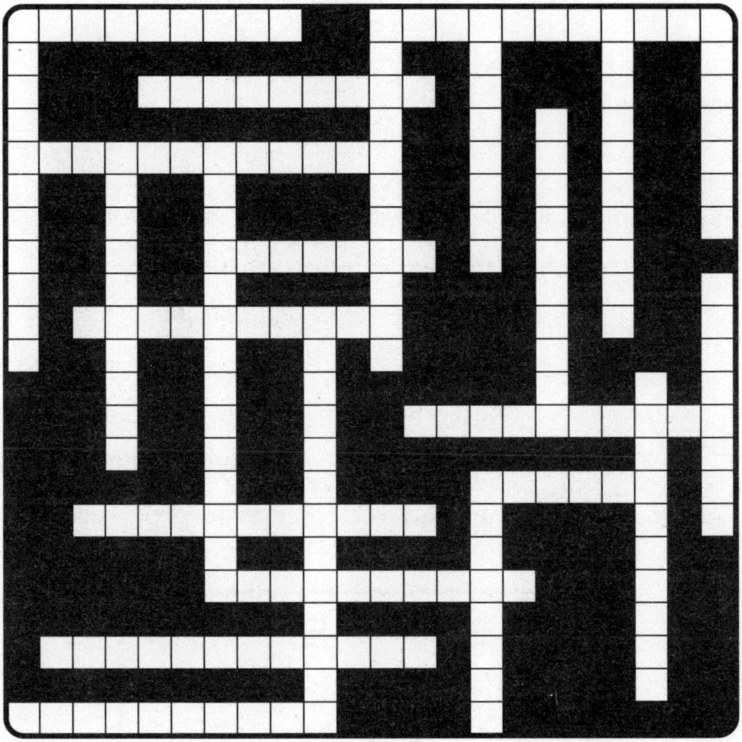

~ 7 ~

WORD SEARCH: DANCE TERMS

Find all the following dance terms in the word search. In the remaining squares another dance term is hidden. What is it?

Arch turn	Fleckerl	Heel turn	Samba roll
Chaîné	Gancho	New Yorker	Shimmy
Chassé	Heel lead	Ronde	Volta

F	L	E	C	K	E	R	L	C
R	Y	M	M	I	H	S	L	U
E	D	N	B	A	N	M	O	O
K	A	R	C	H	T	U	R	N
R	E	U	H	C	O	T	A	A
O	L	T	A	H	H	R	B	T
Y	L	L	I	A	C	O	M	L
W	E	E	N	S	N	N	A	O
E	E	E	E	S	A	D	S	V
N	H	H	I	E	G	E	O	N

~ 8 ~

WHAT THEY SAID

What did the following actually say?

1. What did Jake Wood tell Emma Barton?

   'If all else fails, …'

   a) just keep smiling.
   b) just keep dancing.
   c) just wiggle those hips.

2. Pete Wicks at the start of series 22 said, *'It's weird, but my biggest fear …'*

   a) is getting a 1 paddle.
   b) is going up the stairs to the Clauditorium.
   c) is not dancing in sync with the music.

3. Montell Douglas always wanted to do *Strictly*, but added, *'I'm nervous about …'*

   a) the preparations beforehand.
   b) the heels.
   c) wearing a ballgown.

~ 9 ~

WORD LADDER

In many routines the couples move fast around the dance floor, and here's a chance to possibly follow suit. In this word ladder, change one letter at a time to change 'move' into 'fast' – see if you can do it in 'quick steps'.

MOVE

FAST

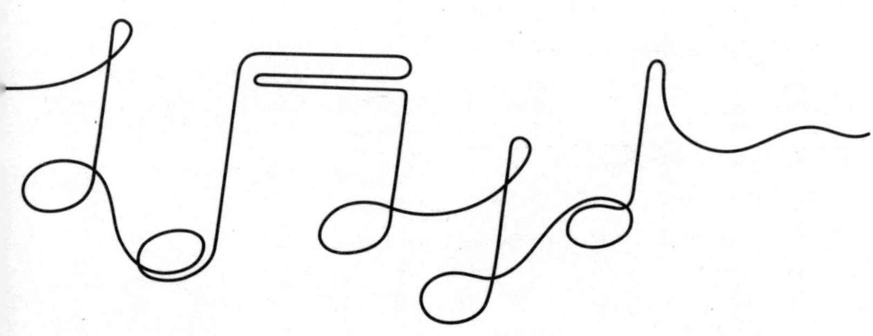

~ 10 ~

FOLLOW THE LEADER

The names of three professional dancers have been entered in the grid below. The individual letters in each of the three names appear in the right order when the grid is followed anti-clockwise, but the names have been mixed together. Starting from the C, bottom right, discover who they are.

O	R	L	A	R	D	Y
O						A
E		R	E	N		M
W		U		U		K
S				A		A
D	N	G	H	E		C

~ 11 ~

CRYPTOGRAM

Solve the cryptogram to discover an interesting observation made by Motsi Mabuse. To give you a start, Z = B, M = P, S = L and T = W.

K	L	F	A	J	■	P	G	■	L	Z	U	N	B
					■			■		B			

J	V	M	O	J	G	G	P	F	E
		P							

H	U	N	O	G	J	S	Q,	■	Z	J	P	F	E
						L	,	■	B				

L	N	B	W	J	F	B	P	A	■	L	F	K
									■			

G	W	U	T	P	F	E	■	T	W	U
			W				■	W		

H	U	N	■	L	O	J
			■			

~ 12 ~

HIDDEN AWAY

Solve the clues correctly and the shaded squares will reveal something that dancers need to choose with great care.

1. Suggest, recommend – and what the judges often do
2. Instantly memorable – like some of Dave Arch's arrangements
3. Not outdoor
4. As shown on the paddles
5. Savour, enjoy

1					
2					
3					
4					
5					

~ 13 ~

TAKE YOUR PICK

1. After watching Debbie McGee perform the Tango, what did Craig Revel Horwood do?

   a) He went over to Debbie McGee and raised her arm in the air in triumph.
   b) He poured a glass of water and raised it in her honour, saying that he wished it was Champagne.
   c) He got on his knees and bowed.

2. In order to pay for his dancing lessons as a young man, Anton used to get up at 3 a.m. – but to do what?

   a) He sorted newspapers at his local newsagent as well as having a delivery round.
   b) He worked as a milkman.
   c) He worked as a baker.

3. *Strictly* has sometimes featured the bandoneon, but what is it?

   a) A South American accordion.
   b) A sparkling headpiece.
   c) A turn in the Argentine Tango.

~ 14 ~

WORD BUILDER

The letters spelling out something that is often seen and enjoyed on *Strictly* have been numbered one to nine. Solve the clues to discover what it is. The answer is two words.

Letters 8, 9, 2 and 5 is to take charge on the dance floor

Letters 7, 2, 3 and 9 give us a foundation

Letters 7, 6, 8 and 5 give us something daring

Letters 4, 1, 2 and 8 give us a whitish gemstone

Letters 1, 2, 5, 5, 8 and 9 give us something held up on *Strictly*

1	2	3	4	5	6	7	8	9

~ 15 ~

CRISS-CROSS: PROFESSIONAL DANCERS

All the following dancers have graced the *Strictly* dance floor and guided their partners well. Find a place for each in the grid below.

7 LETTER NAME

Nancy Xu

8 LETTER NAMES

Erin Boag
Ian Waite

9 LETTER NAMES

Amy Dowden
Neil Jones
Ola Jordan
Oti Mabuse

10 LETTER NAMES

Karen Hardy
Karen Hauer

11 LETTER NAMES

AJ Pritchard
Brendan Cole
Vito Coppola

12 LETTER NAMES

Flavia Cacace
Kevin Clifton
Nicole Cutler
Robin Windsor

13 LETTER NAMES

Dianne Buswell

Matthew Cutler

Vincent Simone

14 LETTER NAMES

Aljaž Škorjanec

Janette Manrara

Jowita Przystał

Nadiya Bychkova

16 LETTER NAME

Michelle Tsiakkas

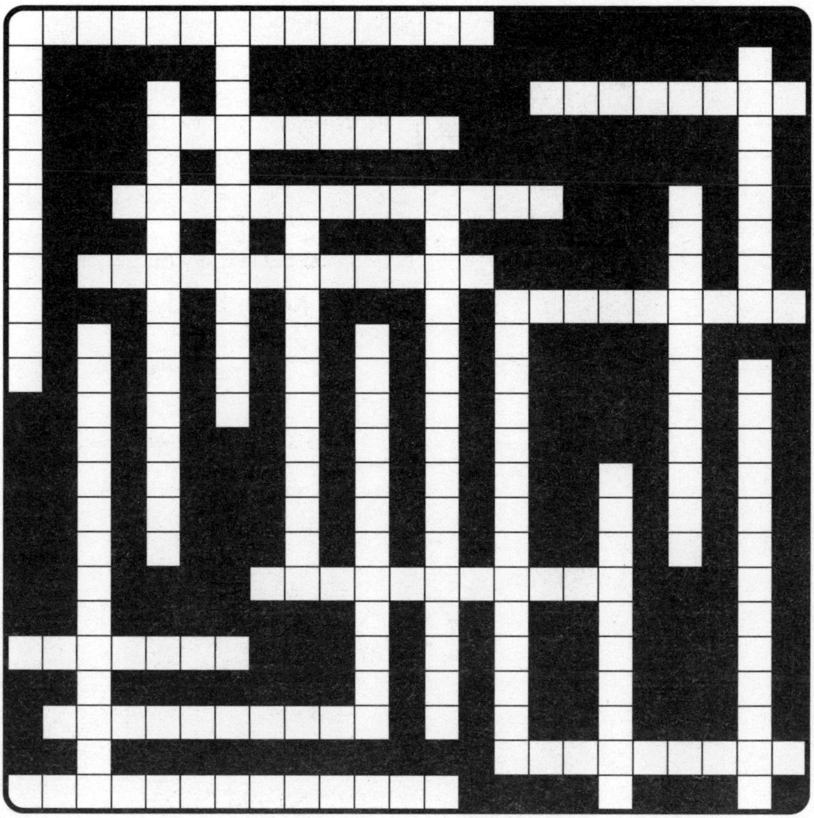

~ *16* ~

STAR NAME

The letters of a name well known to *Strictly* fans have been spread evenly around the circle. Find the first letter of this person's name and follow the letters in order to make up the star – and this person's name. Who is it?

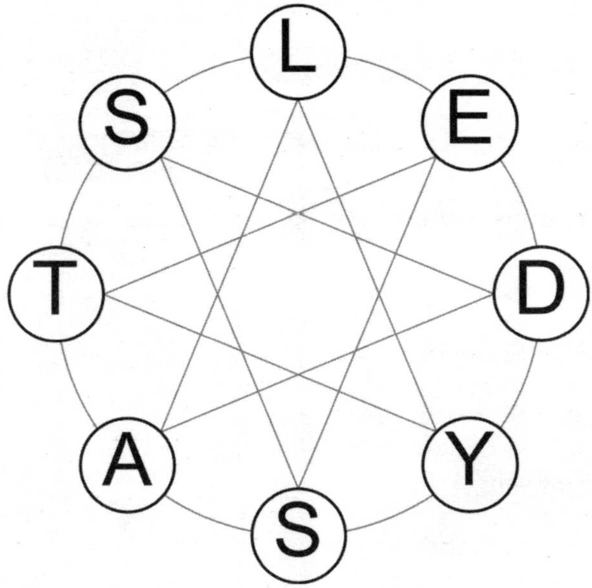

~ 17 ~

WORD LINK

Each of the three word groups in the clues below has a word in common. For example, if the clues were 'spirit', 'crossing' and 'best', the answer would be 'level' ('spirit level', 'level crossing' and 'level best'). Answer each of the following clues correctly and something familiar will be revealed in the shaded column. What is it?

1. water, down, dream
2. fruit, arms, market
3. door, flip, road
4. bar, post, name
5. spell, fish, catch
6. end, south, skin
7. lane, time, food

1			
2			
3			
4			
5			
6			
7			

~ 18 ~

A RIDDLE

My first is in shoe but not in lace,

My second is in hurries, never in haste.

My third is in minute but not in tiny,

My fourth is in polish, never in shiny.

My fifth is in rouge, not in red,

My sixth is in hair but not in head.

And right from Strictly*'s start*

my whole has added a fun part.

What am I?

~ 19 ~

WORD TRACK

Find the starting letter. Then, moving one letter at a time – either horizontally, vertically or diagonally – discover something that is important for dancers to get right.

O	G	R	A
R	E	H	P
O	H	C	Y

~ 20 ~

WORD SEARCH: PIONEERS

When *Strictly* started, Sir Bruce Forsyth said, *'We had no idea the show would take off in the way it did, but we had faith.'* And that faith certainly paid off. In tribute to some of those who took part in the first series, find their names in the grid.

Anton Du Beke
Arlene Phillips
Brendan Cole
Bruce Forsyth
Bruno Tonioli
Christopher Parker
Claire Sweeney
Craig Revel Horwood
David Dickinson
Erin Boag
Jason Wood
Len Goodman
Lesley Garrett
Martin Offiah
Natasha Kaplinsky
Tess Daly
Verona Joseph

D	O	O	W	R	O	H	L	E	V	E	R	G	I	A	R	C	P	K
H	U	S	F	M	A	R	T	I	N	O	F	F	I	A	H	U	T	H
T	T	V	G	G	A	O	B	N	I	R	E	M	A	M	L	H	T	C
Y	A	Q	E	J	S	A	L	I	R	E	C	R	W	D	N	N	E	H
S	N	W	S	R	Q	Z	N	W	L	O	L	S	M	I	O	A	R	R
R	T	A	B	S	O	D	J	B	E	E	A	A	Z	L	S	T	R	I
O	O	P	Q	C	S	N	T	X	N	F	I	H	K	O	N	G	A	S
F	N	H	N	D	D	Z	A	E	G	J	R	J	Z	I	I	K	G	T
E	D	V	E	R	N	K	P	J	O	D	E	E	H	N	K	H	Y	O
C	U	T	J	G	R	H	I	X	O	K	S	X	H	O	C	N	E	P
U	B	N	E	A	I	W	F	B	D	S	W	D	D	T	I	K	L	H
R	E	Q	H	L	S	M	T	W	M	X	E	V	G	O	D	W	S	E
B	K	V	L	X	X	O	H	O	A	J	E	P	V	N	D	O	E	R
E	E	I	R	W	W	X	N	R	N	Y	N	X	H	U	I	O	L	P
H	P	D	B	P	W	R	O	W	K	D	E	S	E	R	V	I	H	A
S	Y	L	A	D	S	S	E	T	O	K	Y	C	X	B	A	N	E	R
Y	Y	R	A	O	S	S	B	T	L	O	E	M	L	R	D	S	O	K
Z	X	B	N	X	E	L	O	C	N	A	D	N	E	R	B	K	I	E
S	N	A	T	A	S	H	A	K	A	P	L	I	N	S	K	Y	B	R

~21~

MINI SUDOKU: LAUGHS

Strictly is full of good humour and has plenty of laughs. In this puzzle, here's a chance for you to delight in more laughs by completing the grid so that every row, column and 2 x 3 box contains the letters that make up the word 'laughs'.

		A		S	
			L		
				G	
	U	H			
H			G		
		S			

~ 22 ~

WORD LADDER

When learning routines, the celebrities have to pay close attention to hand and foot placements and get both right. In this word ladder, change one letter at a time to turn 'hand' into 'foot'.

HAND
FOOT

~ 23 ~

MYSTERY SUDOKU

Complete the grid so that every row, column and 3 × 3 box contains the letters ACEGILNPS in any order. One row or column contains a seven-letter word – one that applies to *Strictly* in more ways than one. What is it?

				S		A	L	P
L	S							
					C	I		S
			S		P	E	G	
	G						P	
	C	I	E		G			
C		A	P					
							E	N
G	E	P		N				

~ 24 ~

CELEBRITY MIX

The names of five *Strictly* celebrities have been split and placed on random jigsaw puzzle pieces. Match the letters below to discover who they are.

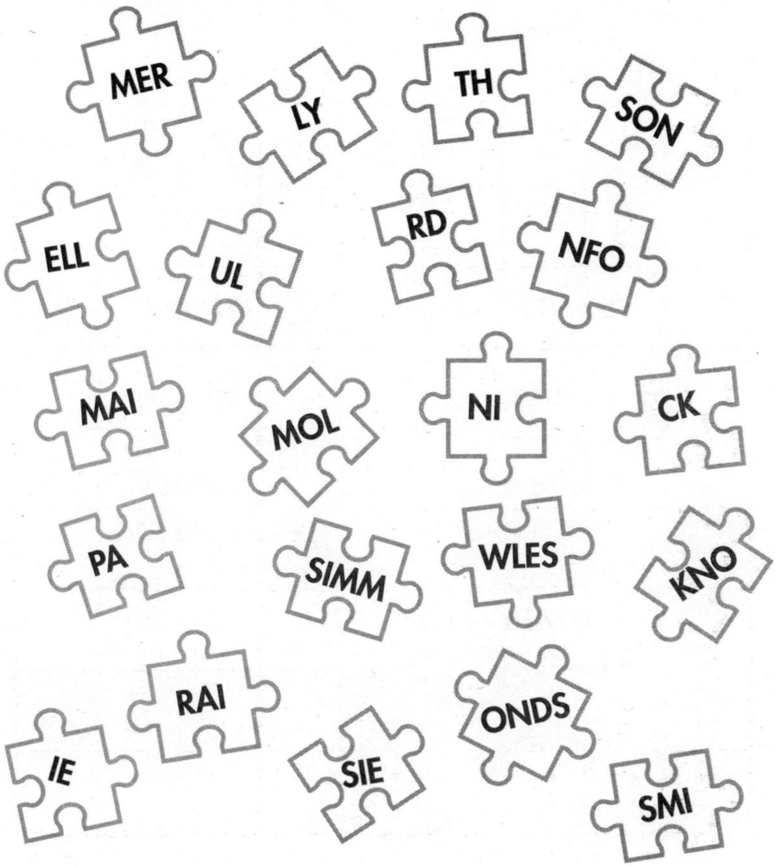

~ 25 ~

CRISS-CROSS

Enter all the following dances, moves and steps into the grid, trying not to get any of the steps out of place.

5 LETTERS
Volta
Weave

6 LETTERS
Gancho
The Hop

8 LETTERS
Arch Turn
Botafogo
Enchufla
Fleckerl
Heel Lead
Lock Step

9 LETTERS
Back Kicks
Cucaracha
New Yorker
Samba Roll

10 LETTERS
Charleston
Quick Jumps

11 LETTERS
Cha Cha Slide
Cuban Breaks
Outside Turn

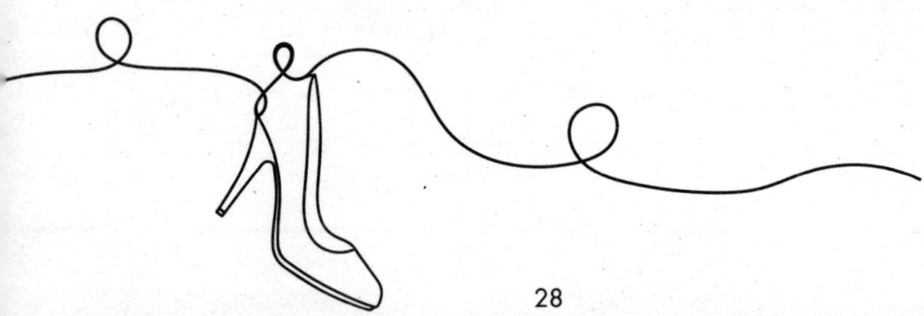

12 LETTERS

American Spin
Chicken Walks
Side Knee Dips
Toe Heel Cross
Two Stage Kick

14 LETTERS

Kick Ball Change

~ 26 ~

LETTER DROP

The letters in each of the columns need to be entered into the squares directly below, but not necessarily in the same order. By placing the letters in the correct squares, you will discover something that Len Goodman said about the fans and followers of *Strictly*.

		E	Y				H				
		T	O	E	B	S	A	N	T		
T	E	C	H	T	A	R	A	T	W	H	F
H	H	A	R	R	E	E	E	O	D	O	E
				■				■			
■	■					■				■	■
									■		
■	■				■					■	■

~ 27 ~

STRICTLY CONUNDRUMS

1. There were fifteen celebrities competing in *Strictly*. All but eight were eliminated. How many were left?

2. How is it possible for Ellie to stand behind Vito, and Vito to stand behind Ellie *at the same time*?

~ 28 ~

A-MAZE-ING

Every series has its twists and turns and here is your chance to enjoy some twists and turns as you work your way from the top of the maze to the bottom.

~ 29 ~

CRYPTOGRAM

Solve the cryptogram to reveal some advice that *Strictly* competitor Fleur East gave to her fellow celebrities. To give you a start, A = Y, Y = K, S = B and I = P.

X	P	R	F	A
				Y

A	F	M	H	N	X	J	Q		B	P	K
Y											

K	F	P	'U		U	G	Z	P	Y
			'						K

B	S	F	M	U		Z	U		B	N		B
	B											

O	F	W	I	X	U	Z	U	Z	F	P
			P							

~ *30* ~

ANAGRAMS

Unscramble the following to reveal the names of *Strictly* presenters and judges.

1. As styled
2. Include a main walk
3. Oh! Reward cool giver
4. Really! Ah bliss!
5. Miss out beam

~ 31 ~

A PERPLEXING POSER

How many d's are on this page?

The judges and audience delighted in the additional dance moves demonstrated in the different and varied routines performed on Saturday.

~ 32 ~

CROSS OUT

Cross out all the letters that appear more than once. The remaining letters, reading from top to bottom and left to right, will spell out something that is often seen and enjoyed on *Strictly*. What is it?

G	P	C	V	I	B	H	M
O	F	S	Q	U	D	X	J
B	X	N	K	Y	C	R	E
H	W	M	J	F	V	O	U
E	R	D	Q	P	G	A	S
N	L	Y	T	C	Z	K	I

~ 33 ~

FOLLOW THE LEADER

The names of three *Strictly* celebrities have been entered in the grid below. The individual letters in each of the three names appear in the right order when the grid is followed anti-clockwise, but the names have been mixed together. Starting from the J, bottom right, discover who they are.

I	W	R	E	G	A	T
A						B
I		N	S	A		E
L		D		L		S
H				K		P
L	H	C	A	D		J

~34~

WORD SEARCH: MUSIC

All the following arrangements of popular songs have featured in *Strictly*. Once you have found them all, the remaining squares hide another famous song that has featured on the show. What is this song, and who wrote it?

Africa	End of Time	Insomnia	Perfect
Bamboleo	Faith	Marry You	Proud Mary
Belle	Fashion	My Girl	Samba
Dynamite	Fever	Pata Pata	Tangier

R	U	O	Y	Y	R	R	A	M	I	R
E	P	E	R	F	E	C	T	Y	M	E
I	S	T	T	I	I	L	O	R	L	V
G	M	I	S	R	N	F	E	A	P	E
N	Y	M	F	E	S	A	L	M	A	F
A	G	A	T	L	O	S	O	D	T	S
T	I	N	A	L	M	H	B	U	A	A
N	R	Y	D	E	N	I	M	O	P	M
I	L	D	N	B	I	O	A	R	A	B
F	A	I	T	H	A	N	B	P	T	A
E	M	I	T	F	O	D	N	E	A	G

~ 35 ~

WHAT THEY SAID

The following quotes are missing their final words. What did Tess, Claudia and Shirley actually say?

1. Tess Daly considers *Strictly* to be '*feelgood television at its very best and it's …*'

   a) magical to watch and be a part of.
   b) so uplifting.
   c) so full of fun and surprise.

2. Claudia Winkleman said that, *'For me, the show is like being …'*

   a) in a twinkly snow globe.
   b) on a merry-go-round of fun.
   c) in a twirling whirling party.

3. In talking about how to judge celebrities, Shirley Ballas said, '*I'll be looking at the quality of how they move, how they interact with their pro and …*'

   a) how they cope with the different styles of dance.
   b) how they learn, adapt and improve.
   c) what unique attributes they bring to the show.

~ *36* ~

NAME TRACK

Find the starting letter. Then, moving one letter at a time – either horizontally, vertically or diagonally – discover the name of a celebrity who made quite an impact when on *Strictly.*

A	D	S	A
H	L	R	D
H	A	A	N

~ 37 ~

DOMINOES

Rearrange the dominoes to reveal words and names connected with *Strictly*. As an example, when the following dominoes are rearranged, the words Salsa and Tango appear.

A	S	L	A	S
A	G	N	O	T

S	A	L	S	A
T	A	N	G	O

1. Rearrange the dominoes to reveal a popular feature on *Strictly*.

P	O	G	U	R
E	N	D	C	A

2. Rearrange the following dominoes to reveal two names well known to *Strictly*. Who are they?

A	D	H	V	C	R	E	A
E	T	Y	S	L	A	S	D

~ 38 ~

STAR NAME

The letters of the name of a *Strictly* star have been spread evenly around the circle. Find the first letter of this person's name and follow the letters to make up the star – and the star's name. Who is it?

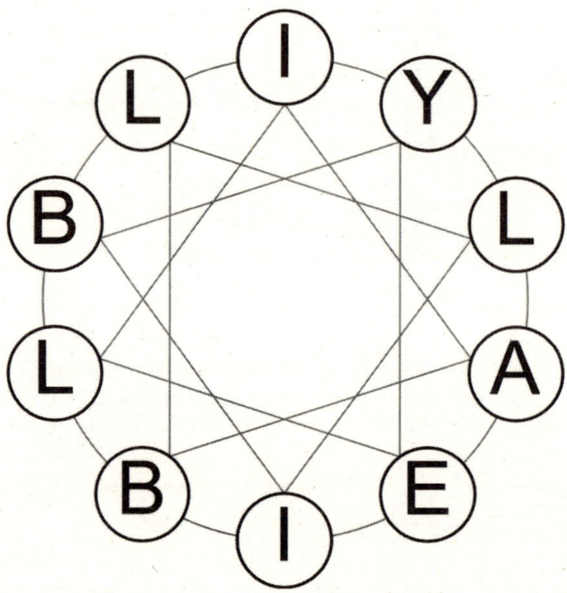

~ 39 ~

HIDDEN WORDS

What dances and dance terms are hidden in the following sentences? As an example, in the sentence, 'In Fiji very many young people have taken up dance,' the hidden dance is Jive (Fi**ji ve**ry).

1. Andy considered adding some additional drum backing to the arrangement.
2. Julian got much laughter on demonstrating his newly learnt steps.
3. Many celebrities found the rehearsal satisfying and could not wait for the actual show to begin.
4. The celebrities got very excited as they began choosing their costumes for the next show.
5. While in Blackpool, Claudia enjoyed a mocha in every café she went to.
6. As a novice dancer, her progressing so far in *Strictly* was a real feat. Her steps and poise were particularly praised.

~40~

MINI SUDOKU: BANTER

There is always a great deal of banter on *Strictly*, especially between the judges, and it all adds to the fun. In this puzzle, here's a chance for you to delight in some banter by completing the grid so that every row, column and 2 x 3 box contains the letters that make up the word 'banter'.

A					B
		R			
		E			R
				A	
R			T		
	N			B	

~ 41 ~

DOWN WORD

Place a three-letter word in the spaces in each row to complete a six-letter word. When the grid is completed correctly, a new word will be formed in the shaded squares: this is something that is seen and encouraged on *Strictly*. What is it?

			H	E	M
			S	O	N
			A	C	E
			S	A	W
			D	O	M
			U	R	N

~ 42 ~

CRISS-CROSS: FINALISTS

All the following were *Strictly* runners up and all came so close to winning the prized Glitterball. Find a place for each in the grid below.

4 LETTER NAME

HRVY

6 LETTER NAME

JB Gill

7 LETTER NAMES

Joe Sugg

Zoe Ball

8 LETTER NAME

Danny Mac

9 LETTER NAMES

Fleur East

Matt Baker

10 LETTER NAMES

Ali Bastian

Emma Barton

Jamie Laing

John Whaite

Matt Dawson

11 LETTER NAMES

Debbie McGee

Julian Clary

Lisa Snowdon

Maisie Smith

Susanna Reid

Tasha Ghouri

12 LETTER NAMES

Bobby Brazier

Colin Jackson

Karim Zeroual

Kellie Bright

Sarah Hadland

13 LETTER NAMES

Ashley Roberts

Chelsee Healey

Molly Rainford

14 LETTER NAMES

Alexandra Burke

Layton Williams

17 LETTER NAME

Christopher Parker

~ 43 ~

A RIDDLE

My first is in party but not in dress,

My second is in more, never in less.

My third is found in hide but not in seek,

My fourth is in strength, never in weak.

My fifth is in smile, not in grin

And my whole will help celebrities win.

What am I?

~ 44 ~

MATCH

Strictly has drawn on some of the best professional dancers from around the world to partner the celebrities. Match the dancer to their country of origin.

1. Vito Coppola	a) Australia
2. Michelle Tsiakkas	b) South Africa
3. Lauren Oakley	c) China
4. Johannes Radebe	d) Ukraine
5. Dianne Buswell	e) Cyprus
6. Nadiya Bychkova	f) Russia
7. Carlos Gu	g) Italy
8. Luba Mushtuk	h) England

~ 45 ~

CODEWORD

Each letter of the alphabet has been replaced by a number. To solve the puzzle, you must decide which letter is represented by which number. To help you start, one of the words has been partly filled in. When you have solved the code, complete the bottom grid to discover something Tess Daly said about *Strictly*. What is it?

1	2	3	4	5	6	7	8	9 T	10	11	12	13
14 E	15 L	16	17	18	19	20	21	22	23	24	25	26

16	5	12	■	16	19	15	4	■	17	26	14	19	2	17

21	13	■	20	16	4

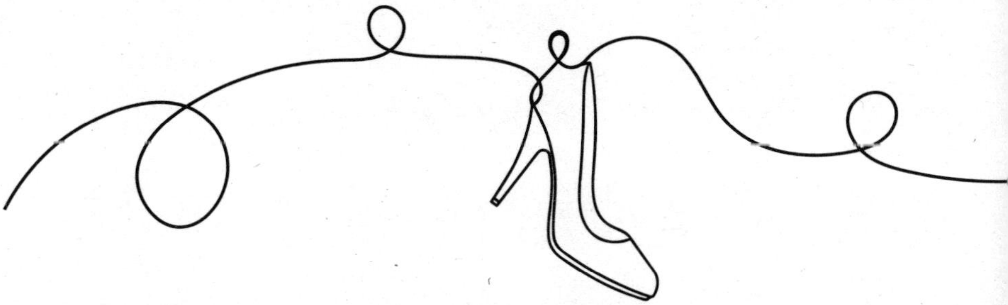

24	16	11	23	17	12	14		13	7	21	3	3	14	3
16		17		26		25		1				17		21
13	17	15	13	17		23	13	14	5	3	16	19	4	11
9		17		21		14		14		12		24		15
5	19	21	16	19		24	16	23	23	21	24	14		4
11		13				9		3		2			20	
14	20	14	24	9	13		22	16	5	9	21	8	5	14
	21			5		13		26		14			13	
16	18	14	12	12	17	9	14		17	3	17	23	9	13
	14			11		12		13				17		17
15		9	6	16	9	21	11	14		23	14	3	17	15
17		14		21		24		19		12		3		5
9	14	11	23	15	17	9	14	13		21	19	15 L	14 E	9 T
21		23				15		14		10		14		14
19	16	16	19	3	17	4		3	12	14	13	13	14	3

~ 46 ~

ANAGRAMS

Unscramble the following to reveal the names of five *Strictly* celebrities: two former politicians and three sports personalities.

1. Demand nice bow
2. Sad bell
3. Today's man
4. Ran noble fact
5. Smiled on smile

~ 47 ~

WORD SEARCH

Hopefully without leading you a dance,
find all the following:

American Smooth
Ballroom
Cha-Cha-Cha
Charleston
Foxtrot
Jive
Lindy Hop
Paso Doble
Quickstep
Rumba
Salsa
Samba
Tango
Viennese Waltz

Z T L A W E S E N N E I V K N
D F U L H D P G M L S T Z M J
J B M P T N N O B S R A P C A
M V R M O W Y O Z C G A L F J
B H X V O V D Q Y N B Q M S U
B T P V M O Y F I M Q L M Y A
E V I J S G M F A U S N T S G
B L D A N X T S I K L O X A G
Y I P K A M O O R L L A B V T
C N A R C H A R L E S T O N A
J D B O I P E T S K C I U Q N
X Y M B R I L U V E W J I Y G
K H U R E W T O R T X O F W O
R O R C M L C H A C H A C H A
T P I N A Z Y N X Z H L P W N

~48~

CROSSED WORDS

Using each of the letters provided in the grid, fill in the squares to form terms often heard on *Strictly*, with one part reading across and the other downwards. In the example below, the letters in the grid can be inserted in the squares to make 'Head Judge'.

A **D** E E G H J U

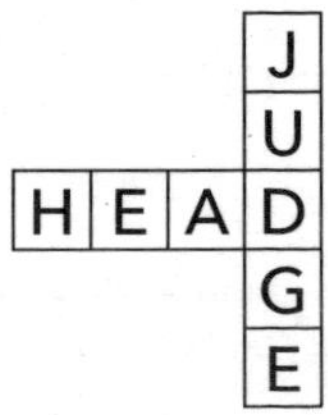

1.

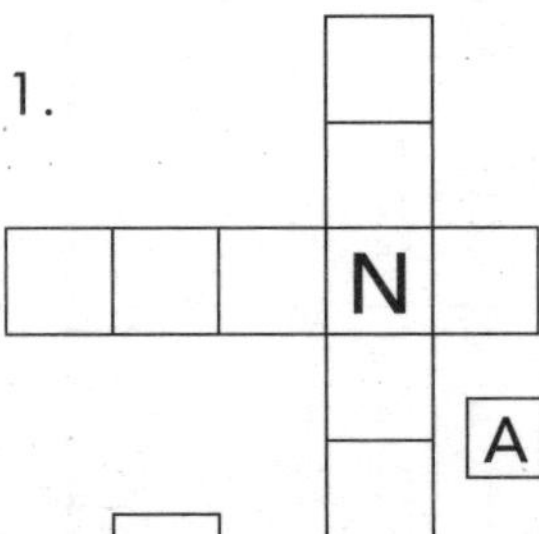

A A D F G I L **N** R

2.

C C C E E H I L **O** P S U

~ 49 ~

CELEBRITY MIX

The names of five *Strictly* celebrities have been split and placed on random jigsaw puzzle pieces. Match the letters below to discover who they are.

~50~

MYSTERY SUDOKU

Complete the grid so that every row, column and 3 x 3 box contains the letters AEHKLOPRS in some order. One row or column contains a seven-letter word very applicable to *Strictly*. What is the mystery word?

H	P	O	S				E	
	L					H		R
E								
		K		A				
L			K	P	S			O
				O		P		
								A
S		E					H	
	R				A	O	S	E

~ *51* ~

LETTER DROP

The letters in each of the columns need to be entered into the squares directly below, but not necessarily in the same order. By placing the letters in the correct squares, you will discover something Chris McCausland said on winning *Strictly*.

			D	U	P	T			C		W							
			T	U	I	P	G	M	T	A	N		I	O	P			
	T		S	H	R	T	R	S	H	T	A	S	D	N	I			
A	O	Y	J	E	S	N	O	R	I	N	Y	N	H	A	D	T	E	
I	N	P	P	O	T	E	U	N	I	O	A	T	A	W	N	P	H	N
		■					■						■					■
■												■				■	■	■
■	■	■								■				■	■	■	■	■
■	■	■													'	■	■	■
								■				■						

~ 52 ~

DOWN THE MIDDLE

Complete all the following words correctly and the shaded squares will reveal something that celebrities need to learn and get right. What is it?

L	I		T	S
S	T		L	E
A	R		M	A
D	E		E	R
L	O		E	R
S	C		R	E
M	E		I	T
P	O		E	R

~ 53 ~

TAKE AWAY

The name of a celebrity has been merged with their professional dancing partner. Take away one to find the other.

1. AKNATTIEODNDEURBHEAKME
2. BDOIBABNYNEBBURASZWEILERL
3. MOCALRLOLYRASINGFOURD
4. KJOATEMYCAJFAODNDEESN
5. TAOMFMLYEDTOCWHDEERN

~ 54 ~

CRYPTOGRAM

Solve the cryptogram to reveal an observation from Anton Du Beke. To give you a start, B = M, E = P and L = G.

P	F	S	S	A	K	K	B	■	H	T	■	X	Z	K
							M	■			■			

E	J	K	E	S	J	■	N	F	V	O	H	V	L
P			P			■							G

X	K	L	J	X	U	J	A	■	X	K
		G						■		

B	Y	T	H	O,	■	X	K	Y	O	U	H	V	L
M				,	■								G

H	V	■	E	J	A	G	J	O	X
		■	P						

U	F	A	B	K	V	I

~ *55* ~

TAKING THE LEAD

Starting with the circled letter and moving one letter at a time, either horizontally or vertically, find the names of four celebrities who all made an impact on series 22.

(S)	A	N	D	E	B	O
A	R	A	J	I	T	R
H	D	L	A	M	H	W
H	A	U	P	K	C	I
M	A	N	K	K	N	O
K	S	H	C	I	S	W
R	I	A	N	N	E	L

~ 56 ~

WORD BUILDER

The letters spelling out something that is important to the success of the celebrities, and the show itself, have been numbered one to nine. Solve the clues to discover what it is.

Letters 5, 7 and 3 give us a tree

Letters 1, 8, 6 and 2 give us something unusual

Letters 6, 4, 5 and 9 give us something genuine

Letters 3, 2, 8 and 9 help to make better

Letters 4, 1, 5, 7 and 2 is to delete

1	2	3	4	5	6	7	8	9

~ 57 ~

SPECIAL FEATURE

Solve the clues – then rearrange the letters that appear in the shaded squares to reveal an exciting feature of *Strictly*.

1. Dance from the Roaring Twenties
2. *Strictly* studio
3. Movement made by Lindy?
4. *Strictly* winner Ore
5. Saucy Latin dance
6. American who does a four-beat step
7. Ms Buswell
8. Tango from Buenos Aires
9. From Vienna, the oldest of ballroom dances

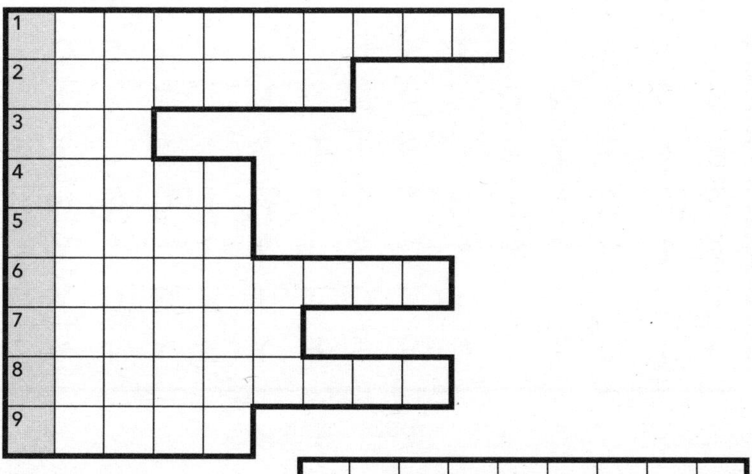

~ 58 ~

WORD SEARCH

In this word search there is just one word to find – *Strictly*. But where exactly is it?

S	L	T	I	S	R	C	T	R	I	L	C	T	I	Y
T	Y	R	T	Y	T	S	S	R	L	T	R	S	L	L
L	I	I	S	T	S	T	C	Y	L	I	S	I	Y	I
R	Y	R	C	T	L	R	Y	T	L	S	C	L	C	L
S	T	Y	I	R	C	T	Y	S	T	L	R	T	R	S
R	I	S	T	R	S	T	C	Y	S	Y	L	Y	C	Y
T	C	R	R	I	T	L	S	Y	R	I	L	S	R	I
R	L	Y	I	S	C	Y	T	S	L	C	L	Y	C	T
S	R	R	L	I	T	R	L	Y	I	Y	Y	S	C	R
T	T	S	R	C	I	R	R	Y	R	I	T	Y	I	T
I	C	T	Y	S	L	S	I	S	S	I	Y	L	T	S
R	Y	L	S	I	R	T	L	C	R	I	C	S	R	I
C	L	S	T	R	L	C	S	I	T	R	T	Y	Y	C
C	I	Y	C	L	I	T	C	T	I	L	S	C	Y	T
Y	L	S	T	I	C	S	T	R	Y	S	Y	I	Y	L

~ 59 ~

THE A LIST

All the following *Strictly* celebrities have had the letter 'a' removed from their names. Who are they?

1. Dmpety
2. Mrkrmprksh
3. Dnnymc
4. Srhhdlnd
5. Hmzyssin
6. Libstin
7. Nstci
8. Shynewrd
9. Nglscnlon
10. Jydedms
11. Dnwlker
12. Clrmfo

~ 60 ~

A RIDDLE

My first is in style but not in look,

My second is in novel, never in book.

My third is in heel but not in lift,

My fourth is in present, never in gift.

My fifth is in large but not in small,

My sixth is in party, never in ball.

And my whole is very much needed and seen

whenever Strictly *is on the screen.*

What am I?

~ 61 ~

NAME TRACK

Find the starting letter. Then, moving one letter at a time – either horizontally, vertically or diagonally – discover the name of a celebrity who enjoyed and did so well on *Strictly*.

S	S	A	J
E	Y	M	G
N	I	U	C

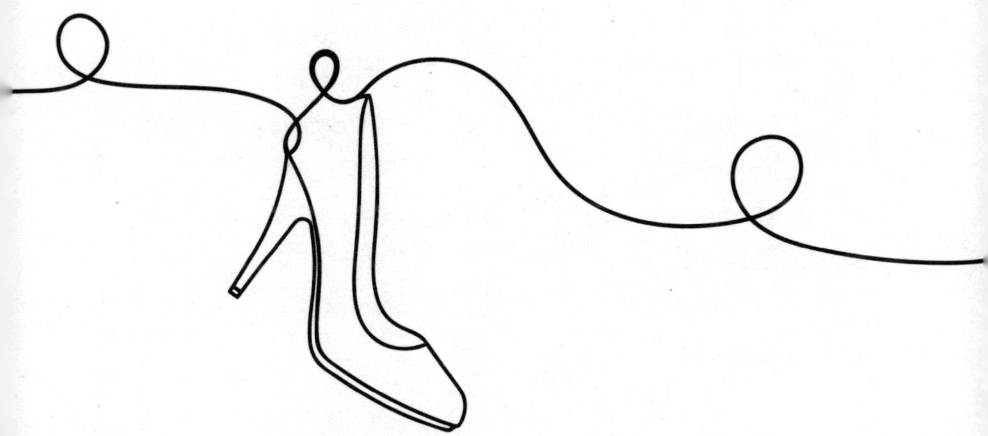

~ *62* ~

CROSSWORD: ON FIRST NAME TERMS

The answers are the first names of all the following celebrities.

ACROSS

3. __ Wise (4)
5. __ Brook (5)
6. __ West (5)
7. __ Brazier (5)
11. __ Harman (5)
12. __ Bye (5)
13. __ Evans (5)
15. __ Yassin (5)
17. __ Castle (6)
18. __ Hingis (7)
19. __ Griffin (3)
20. __ Rainford (5)
23. __ Walker (3)
24. __ Goss (4)
25. __ Wicks (4)
26. __ Quek (3)

DOWN

1. __ Mellor (4)
2. __ Quentin (8)
3. __ Logan (5)
4. __ Jones (4)
5. __ Adams (4)
6. __ Chambers (3)
8. __ Bailey (4)
9. __ Lunghi (6)
10. __ Krishan (5)
12. __ Whaite (4)
14. __ Williams (6)
16. __ Rippon (6)
17. __ Peaty (4)
21. __ Oduba (3)
22. __ Dennis (3)

~ 63 ~

CROSS OUT

Cross out all the letters that appear more than once. The remaining letters, reading from top to bottom and left to right, will spell out something seen and used on *Strictly*. What is it?

C	H	B	R	O	F	Z	G
L	D	J	W	S	Y	N	V
T	M	X	G	I	Z	H	D
R	Q	V	C	A	L	B	W
O	K	H	E	T	D	S	Y
J	U	F	X	N	P	I	Q

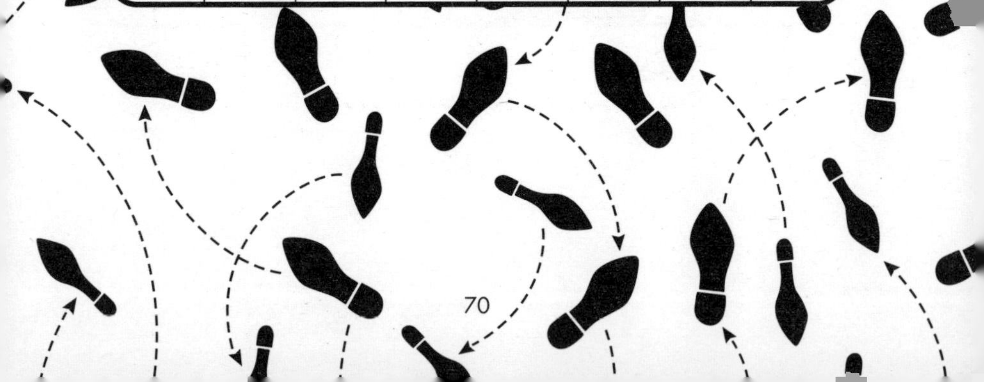

~ *64* ~

FOLLOW THE LEADER

Three names well known to *Strictly* fans have been entered in the grid below. The individual letters in each of the three names appear in the right order when the grid is followed anti-clockwise, but the names have been mixed together. Starting from the M, bottom right, discover who they are.

E	I	U	S	O	E	T
R						Z
M		L	T	S		L
E		E		L		O
A				S		F
B	A	B	A	U		M

~ *65* ~

BETWEEN THE LINES

Something special that is enjoyed on *Strictly* can be inserted in the middle line so that, reading downwards, nine three-letter words are formed. What is it?

S	S	A	P	C	E	F	N	A
Y	T	L	Y	T	E	W	T	D

~ 66 ~

MINI SUDOKU: TWIRLS

Many a routine sees twists and twirls and this puzzle highlights the twirls. Complete the grid so that every row, column and 2 x 3 box contains the letters that make up the word 'twirls'.

	R				
		T			L
			S		
S				W	
		L			R
			I		

~67~

CRISS-CROSS

All the following nobly took part in some of the earlier series of *Strictly* and helped make it become a success and the spectacle that it remains today. Find a place for each name in the grid.

7 LETTER NAME

Sid Owen

8 LETTER NAME

DJ Spoony

9 LETTER NAMES

Alex Jones

Dave Myers

Jerry Hall

Jodie Kidd

10 LETTER NAMES

Ali Bastian

Gary Rhodes

Mark Benton

Mark Foster

Matt Dawson

11 LETTER NAMES

Anita Dobson

Laila Rouass

Rachel Riley

12 LETTER NAMES

Carol Smillie

Dennis Taylor

Jason Donovan

Ricky Whittle

Robbie Savage

14 LETTER NAMES

Kimberley Walsh

Michael Vaughan

16 LETTER NAME

Michelle Williams

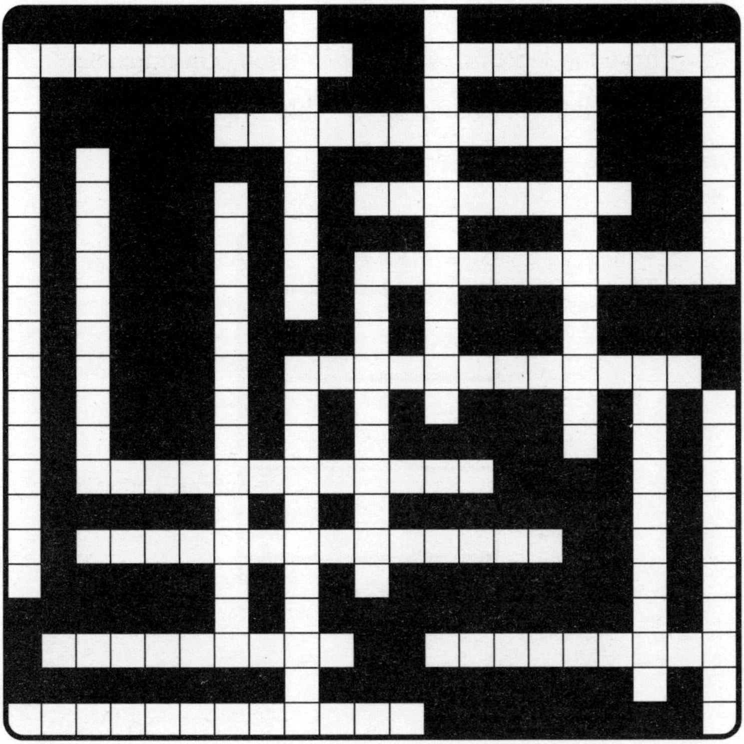

~ 68 ~

WORD LADDER

In dancing the Rumba, the hip movement comes from the leg and, with this in mind, change one letter at a time to turn 'hip' into 'leg'.

HIP

LEG

~ 69 ~

ONE FROM THE OTHER

The letters of two words have been combined into a single line. The letters of each word remain in sequence and both words are of equal length. Discover one word to reveal the other. All the words relate to *Strictly*. As an example, in

RIFASLEL

the two combined words are 'rise' and 'fall'.

1. DSATEPNCSE
2. GDRAONCUEP
3. ATRURCNH
4. HLEEEALD
5. CWUABALKNS

~ 70 ~

SENTENCE GRAM

Some of the words in the following sentence have been turned into anagrams and these are shown in italics. Solve the anagrams to make sense of the sentence.

The *overall sum* __________ work of the *bare word* ________ department was very important in the *real share* _________ and the *carthorse* __________ was also much involved in preparing for *tidy calming concerts* __________.

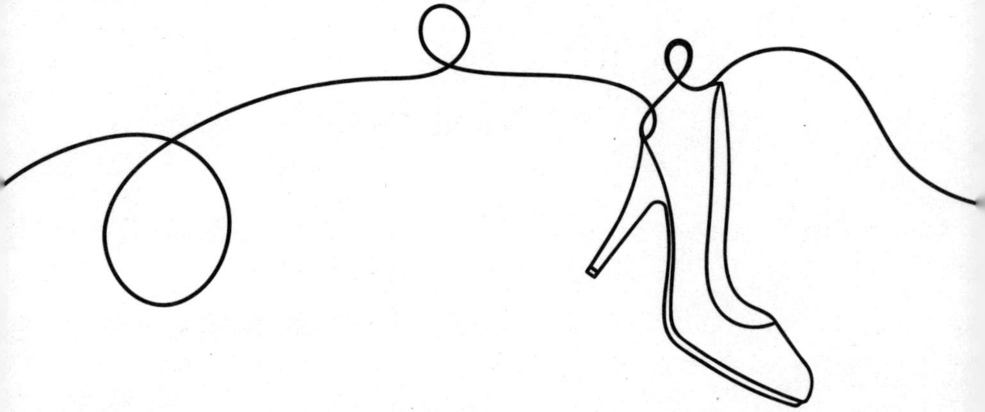

~ 71 ~

WORD LINK

Each of the three word groups in the clues below has a word in common. For example, if the clues were 'spirit', 'crossing' and 'best', the answer would be 'level' ('spirit level', 'level crossing' and 'level best'). Answer each of the following clues correctly to discover an important consideration for each dance and something that needs to be got right. What is it?

1. home, sure, worse
2. take, time, spare
3. secret, air, day
4. order, straw, minute
5. cause, long, touch

1			
2			
3			
4			
5			

~ 72 ~

STAR NAME

The letters of the name of a *Strictly* star have been spread evenly around the circle. Find the first letter of this person's name and follow the letters in order to make up the star – and the star's name. Who is it?

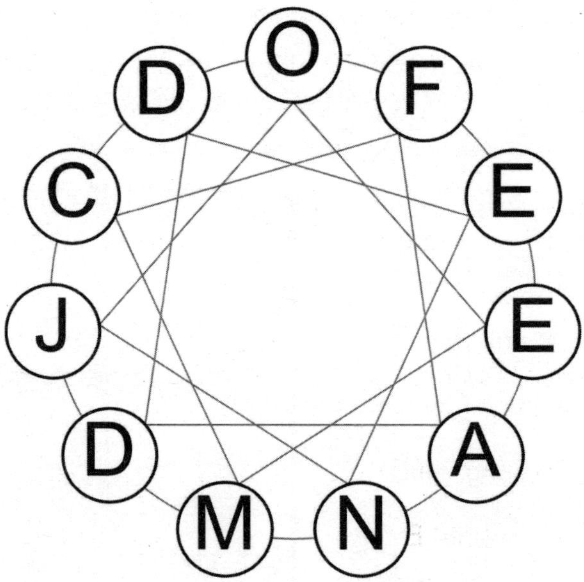

~ 73 ~

TAKE YOUR PICK

1. Shortly before dancing and winning the 2016 *Strictly* final, what happened to Ore Oduba?
   a) He had a nosebleed.
   b) He got terrible cramp in his thighs.
   c) He accidentally locked himself out of his dressing room.

2. When dancing the Cha Cha to 'Could It Be Magic', magician Paul Daniels performed a trick with his dance partner Ola Jordan. What did he do?
   a) At the end of the routine Paul produced a bouquet of feathered flowers which he presented to Ola.
   b) Paul produced a silk handkerchief, threw it in the air and as it descended, it changed into a shower of silk petals.
   c) Paul showed an empty box which Ola then magically appeared from.

3. Cuban violinist Enrique Jorrin composed the first Cha Cha song but what did he name the term after?
   a) He thought it best described the sound of the rhythm.
   b) The shuffling sound the dancers' shoes made on the floor.
   c) A bird he had heard making a 'cha-cha' sound which inspired him to write the song.

~ 74 ~

CRYPTOGRAM

Solve the cryptogram to discover one of the things Craig Revel Horwood believes that *Strictly* demonstrates. To give you a start, Z = C, G = V and V = D.

O	P	■	E	H	Y	■	J	C	C	A	E
		■				■					

E	H	Y	X	M	K	A	P	■	E	H	Y
								■			

Z	J	L	■	J	Z	S	Y	J	A	A	E
C			■		C						

O	D	C	X	H	G	K	■	J	M
					V		■		

D	J	L	E	■	C	K	H	C	A	K
				■						

W	J	G	K	■	V	H	L	K
		V		■	D			

~ 75 ~

CROSS OUT

Cross out all the letters that appear more than once. The remaining letters, reading from top to bottom and left to right, will spell out something judges look out for and appreciate. What is it?

D	G	A	R	H	B	M	F
K	P	J	N	C	O	Q	I
U	M	H	V	Z	K	X	W
C	X	S	A	G	P	H	B
J	F	O	U	I	T	D	Q
W	Y	R	L	V	N	E	Z

~ 76 ~

A-MAZE-ING

Every week the celebrities and professional dance partners aim for a good position on the leaderboard. In this maze, work your way from the bottom of the leaderboard to the top. Good luck!

~ 77 ~

MAKING AN ENTRANCE

First impressions go a long way in a *Strictly* routine, and some celebrities have been involved in spectacular openings. Match the celebrity to the opening they made.

1. Jamie Borthwick	a) flying in on a bike
2. Ann Widdecombe	b) descended from a clock
3. Russell Grant	c) emerged from an octopus
4. Scott Mills	d) descended on a bottle of ketchup
5. Victoria Pendleton	e) appeared on a *Titanic*-like balcony
6. Chris McCausland	f) perched on a crescent moon
7. Georgia May Foote	g) emerged as a crab
8. Joe McFadden	h) fired from a cannon
9. Toyah Willcox	i) emerged from a hot air balloon basket

~ *78* ~

LETTER DROP

The letters in each of the columns need to be entered into the squares directly below, but not necessarily in the same order. By placing the letters in the correct places, you will reveal an interesting thought from Craig Revel Horwood. What is it?

			C					L	M		O		
		N	A	N		W	I	E	I	K	E		
L	A	F	W	N	I	R	T	T	T	P	I		S
D	I	O	E	E	D	S	H	Y	H	H	M	T	A
				■			■					■	
				'	■					■			
■	■				■							■	■
■	■	■				■						■	■

~ *79* ~

WORD LADDER

Whether a ballroom dance or dance in a ballroom, here's a chance to turn, one letter at a time, the word 'ball' into 'room'.

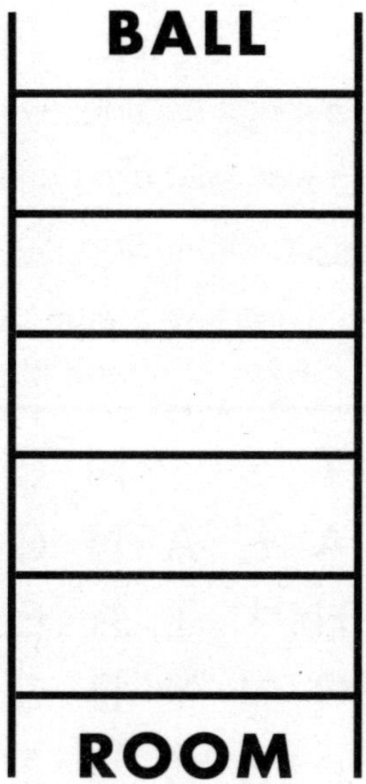

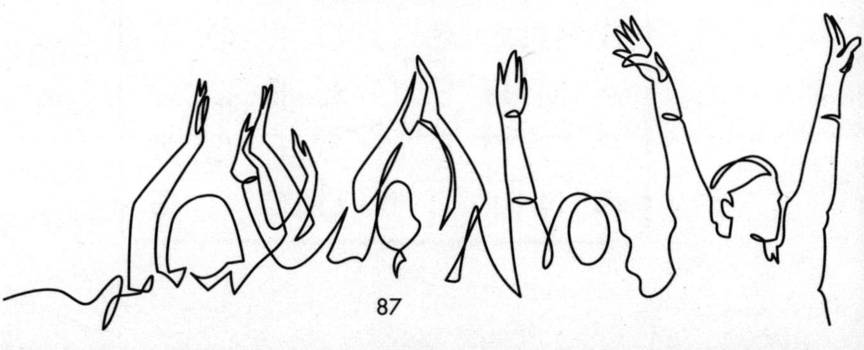

~ 80 ~

WORD SEARCH

This word search is based on some of the things that Head Judge Shirley Ballas is looking for. Each of the underlined words can be found in the grid. The remaining letters, read left to right, top to bottom, will spell out something else Shirley also hopes to see from a contestant.

<u>Great</u> <u>grounding</u> through the <u>floor</u>, with <u>good</u> <u>balance</u>. How they interact with their <u>arms</u> and <u>legs</u>. How they translate the <u>music</u> with their <u>body</u>. Do they have great <u>chemistry</u> with their <u>partner</u>?

Y	R	T	S	I	M	E	H	C
R	B	A	L	A	N	C	E	T
E	C	H	I	T	A	E	R	G
N	I	R	N	Y	D	O	B	K
T	S	L	O	O	U	T	D	S
R	U	I	E	O	D	E	O	T
A	M	H	E	G	L	B	O	O
P	S	M	R	A	S	F	G	X
G	N	I	D	N	U	O	R	G

~ 81 ~

ANAGRAMS

Unscramble the following to reveal the names of five *Strictly* contestants: a sports pundit, an Olympic medallist, a TV personality, a TV presenter and a singer.

1. Lo! Superman
2. Am noted
3. Sweet pick
4. Knew no slick
5. An' envy news

~ 82 ~

MYSTERY SUDOKU

Complete the grid so that every row, column and 3x3 box contains the letters AGHILMORU in some order. One row or column contains a seven-letter word relating to *Strictly*. What is the mystery word?

	A			H				
		R				A		U
		U	A			G	M	
L				R	H			
	I						L	
			U	L				G
	U	G			A	L		
O		M				R		
				G			I	

~ 83 ~

FITTING WORDS

Fit the following words into the grid so that another word is created in the shaded squares – it is something that is needed by all who take part in *Strictly*.

Ballroom	Music	Routine	Tango
Foxtrot	Partner	*Strictly*	

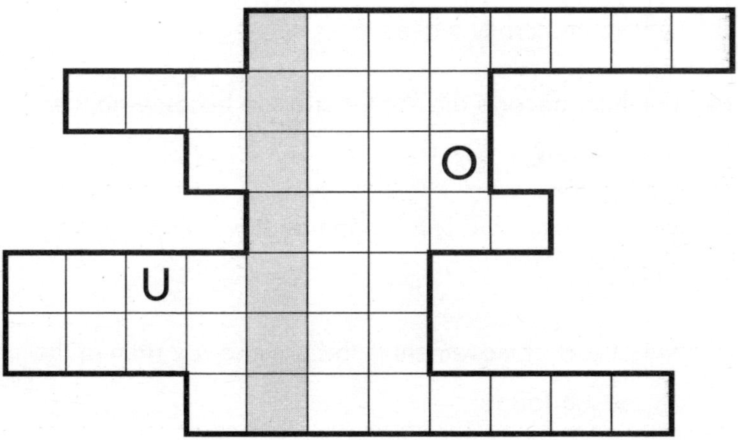

~ 84 ~

TRIVIA

1. In series 6, who did judge Arlene Phillips 'compliment' for '*being outstanding at dancing really badly*'?
2. Ed Balls' 'Gangnam Style' routine made *Strictly* history, but what Latin dance did he perform?
3. Who won the first series of *Strictly*, and also presented part of the second series while Tess Daly was on maternity leave?
4. In which decade did the Charleston become popular in America?
5. What number did Len Goodman have a unique way of saying?
6. What sort of movement is the gancho, as seen in the Argentine Tango?
7. Which popular feature was introduced as part of the competition in *Strictly* series 16?

~ *85* ~

MISSING A LETTER

Each of the following words is missing a letter. Put each missing letter into the grid below to find a name well known to *Strictly* fans.

1. Pro_e
2. S_eet
3. Beg_n
4. Gra_e
5. Awa_e
6. Sha_e
7. St_le
8. Sc_re
9. _atch

1	2	3	4	5	6	7	8	9

~86~

CRISS-CROSS

Just as the dancers must fit their actions to the music, here's a chance to fit the music to the grid. Find a place for each of these popular pieces of music, which have all at some time been danced to on *Strictly*.

4 LETTER TITLES

Hero
Lost

5 LETTER TITLES

Fuego
Shine

6 LETTER TITLES

Africa
Bolero
Closer
Milord

7 LETTER TITLES

Car Wash
Cherish
Fantasy

8 LETTER TITLES

Get Happy
Insomnia
Marry You
Open Arms
Physical
Red Alert
Rescue Me
Time Warp

9 LETTER TITLES

Footloose
Tea for Two
That's Life

10 LETTER TITLE

Canned Heat

11 LETTER TITLES

Crazy in Love

If I Can Dream

Rock the Boat

Stayin' Alive

12 LETTER TITLES

Mack the Knife

Rule the World

14 LETTER TITLE

Love is in the Air

15 LETTER TITLE

California Dreamin'

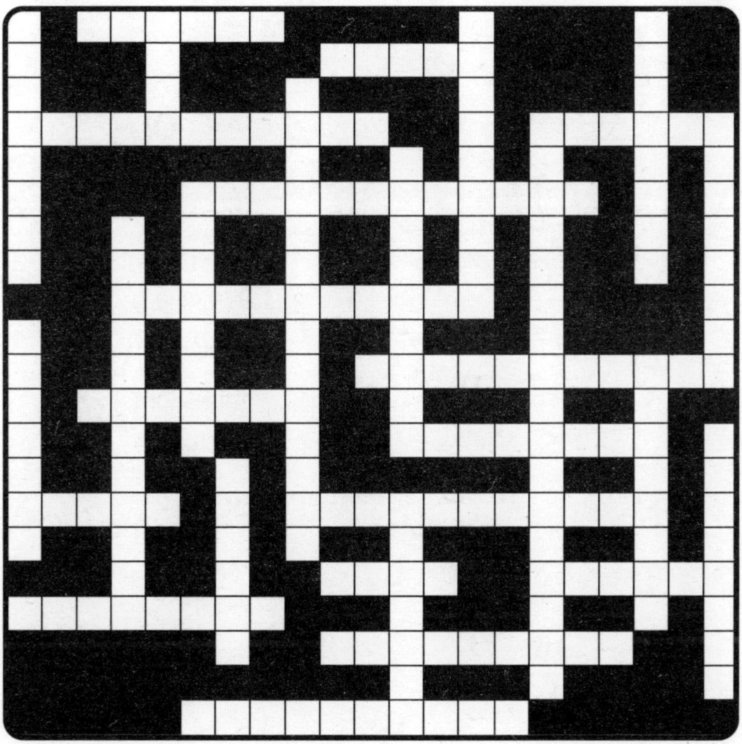

~ *87* ~

CELEBRITY MIX

The names of five *Strictly* celebrities have been split and placed on random jigsaw puzzle pieces. Match the letters below to discover who they are.

~ 88 ~

CROSS OUT

Cross out all the letters that appear more than once. The remaining letters, reading from top to bottom and left to right, will spell out something judges watch very closely on *Strictly*. What is it?

D	H	A	P	V	N	G	J
W	Q	M	R	B	U	O	X
C	V	Z	X	E	K	Y	D
K	G	L	A	U	R	N	P
M	I	H	D	Q	J	F	W
O	C	Y	T	E	S	Z	B

~ 89 ~

WORD SEARCH: CELEBRITY

For many years 15 celebrities have taken part in each series of *Strictly*. The word 'celebrity' appears 15 times in the star below. This word appears either horizontally or vertically, forwards or backwards. Can you find all 15?

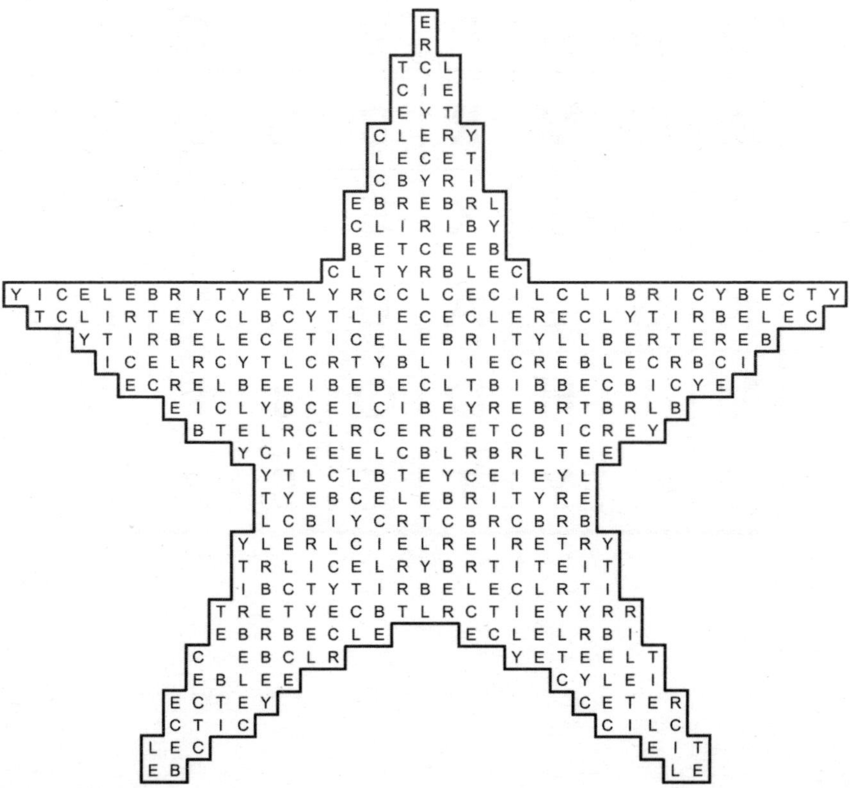

~ 90 ~

MINI SUDOKU: FAMILY

Strictly is very much a family show – and here's a chance to celebrate its family-feel by successfully completing the grid so that every row, column and 2 x 3 box contains the letters that make up the word 'family'.

L	I	M			
					A
		Y	I	F	
				M	
Y			L		

~ 91 ~

CRYPTOGRAM

During his many years as Head Judge on *Strictly*, Len Goodman became well-known for his unsurpassed knowledge of ballroom and Latin dance as well as his quick wit. Solve the cryptogram to discover one of his many amusing comments. To give you a start, D = L, P = C, O = Y and Z = B.

O	B	V		X	D	B	G	M	R	C
Y					L					

G	P	T	B	A	A		M	Y	G	M
	C									

X	D	B	B	T		D	K	U	R
	L					L			

Z	V	M	M	R	T		B	J
B								

G		P	T	V	H	L	R	M
		C						

~ 92 ~

NAME TRACK

Find the starting letter. Then, moving one letter at a time – either horizontally, vertically or diagonally – discover the name of a celebrity who made quite an impact when appearing on *Strictly*.

K	N	H	S
A	A	A	A
L	P	K	T
I	N	S	Y

~ 93 ~

WHAT THEY SAID

The following quotes have some of their words missing. What did they actually say?

1. What did Bruno Tonioli say next? *'The good thing about Strictly is …'*

   a) that you never know what is going to happen.
   b) the celebrities have this great capacity to surprise.
   c) it is sooooo much fun.

2. At the start of series 22, Anton Du Beke was asked about how the celebrities and professionals would be feeling. He replied, *'They won't know …'*

   a) what an amazing journey it is until they take those first steps.
   b) how overwhelming it can feel until they step out on the floor.
   c) what nerves are like until they walk on this floor.

3. What did Kaye Adams say next? *'The only eye I have on the glitterball will be to …*

   a) hope some of its sparkle rubs off on me.
   b) make sure I don't trip over it and smash it by mistake.
   c) not drop it if, by some miracle, I happen to win.

~ 94 ~

WORD LADDER

The Foxtrot is a favourite with many professional dancers. It's an elegant, smooth, gliding dance with timing varying between slow and fast. There is a gentle rise and fall to the dance – and now here's a chance to appreciate this flowing aspect by changing, one letter at a time, the word 'rise' into 'fall'.

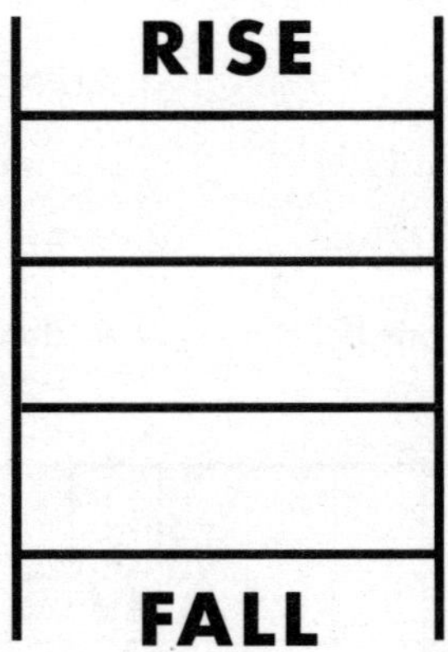

~ 95 ~

ANT-ICIPATING *STRICTLY*

Every time it is on, *Strictly*, with its glamour, glitz and contestants, has the ability to enchant – and this is not the only *ant*-ending word that is relev*ant* to *Strictly*. Solve the clues to discover more *ant*-ending words. When you have all the answers, the shaded squares will spell a mystery word, not an ant-ending word, but one used in, as well as applied to, *Strictly*.

1. An important, meaningful ant (11)
2. A floating ant (7)
3. A perceptive ant (9)
4. An agreeable ant (8)
5. An immediate ant (7)
6. A successful ant (10)
7. A stylish, graceful ant (7)

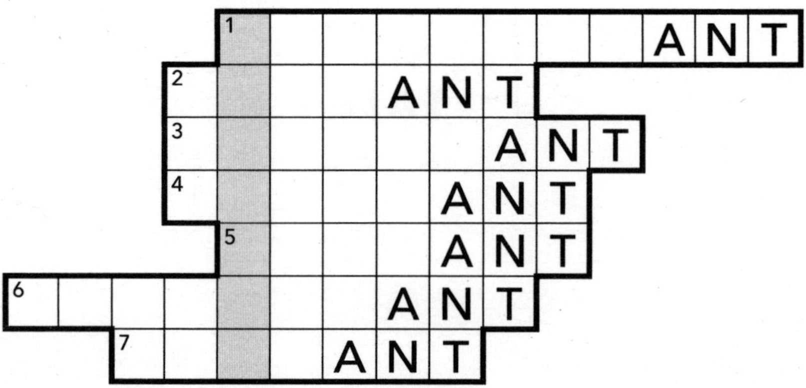

~ 96 ~

STAR NAME

The letters of the name of a *Strictly* star have been spread evenly around the circle. Find the first letter of this person's name and follow the letters in order to make up the star – and the star's name. Who is it?

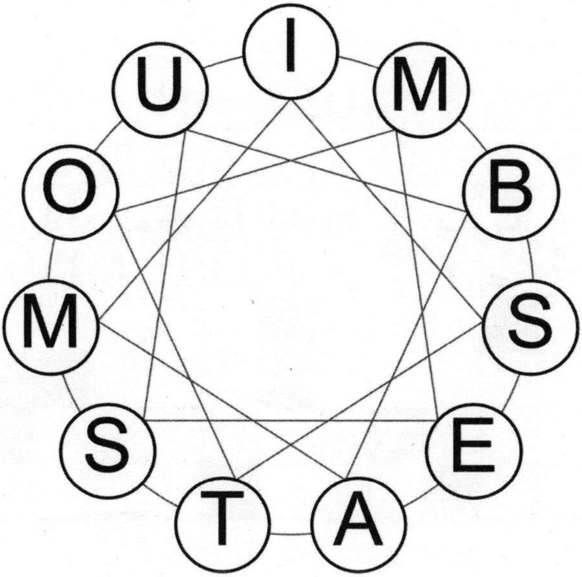

~ 97 ~

LETTER DROP

The letters in each of the columns need to be entered into the squares directly below, but not necessarily in the same order. By placing the letters in the correct squares, you will discover what Ann Widdecombe said after performing her Week 1 waltz.

	T				U			H	L			
	E	H	A	O	S		T	S	D	L		
I	Y	E	U	T	H	H	B	A	I	N	S	
S	F	O	Y	T	S	E	O	U	A	D	K	A
		■				■						■
■					'	■			'	■	■	■
■				■							■	■
			■				■					

~ *98* ~

ANAGRAMS

Unscramble the following to reveal the names of celebrities who have appeared on *Strictly*. What do they all have in common?

1. Has zany aims!
2. Our abode
3. I'm this soul
4. Solely realising
5. Coy, steady, olé!

~ 99 ~

MYSTERY SUDOKU

Complete the grid so that every row, column and 3x3 box contains the letters EHILMPRTU in some order. One row or column contains a seven-letter word – which can also be applied to *Strictly*. What is the mystery word?

	E	T			R	I		
			H		M	R		
I				T			M	
E			P					
	T	M		R		L	P	
					L			I
	M			L				P
		U	T		H			
		I	U			H	L	

~ 100 ~

TAKE YOUR PICK – CRAIG'S PADDLE

Which is the correct answer? Take your pick.

1. At the start of series 22, Craig was reminded he had used his 1 paddle how many times?

    a) eight
    b) ten
    c) twelve

2. During series 22 Craig was invited to the Clauditorium and told he had just awarded his 100th 10 paddle, but to whom?

    a) Tasha Ghouri
    b) Sarah Hadland
    c) JB Gill

3. When Craig was asked what makes a 10, he said *'It means I have nothing to say ...*

    a) – it is faultless.
    b) except it's incredible.
    c) I have just been blown away.

~ 101 ~

CRISS-CROSS

All the following people very much entertained us while on *Strictly* and each of them has their place in the grid below. Where does each fit in?

4 LETTER NAMES

HRVY
Lulu

7 LETTER NAMES

AJ Odudu
Joe Sugg
Sam Quek

8 LETTER NAMES

James Bye
Matt Goss

9 LETTER NAMES

Alex Scott
Dan Walker
Fleur East
Harry Judd
Pete Wicks

10 LETTER NAMES

Bill Bailey
Ellie Leach
Jamie Laing
John Whaite
Peter Andre

11 LETTER NAMES

Alesha Dixon

Darren Gough

12 LETTER NAMES

Angela Rippon

Helen Skelton

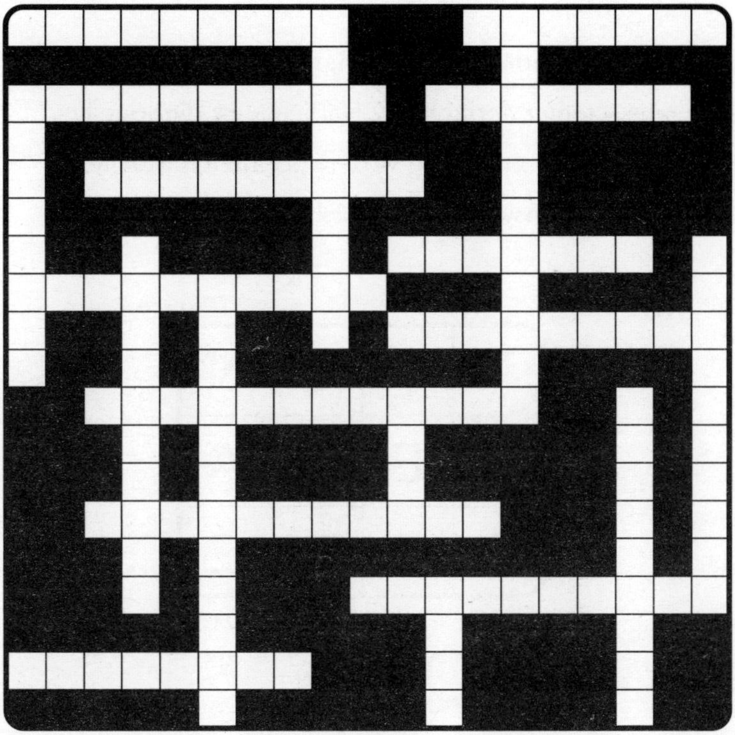

~ *102* ~

ON TRACK

Find the starting letter. Then, moving one letter at a time – either horizontally, vertically or diagonally – discover something very important on *Strictly*. The answer is two words, but what is it?

T	I	C	N
U	E	N	A
O	R	D	E

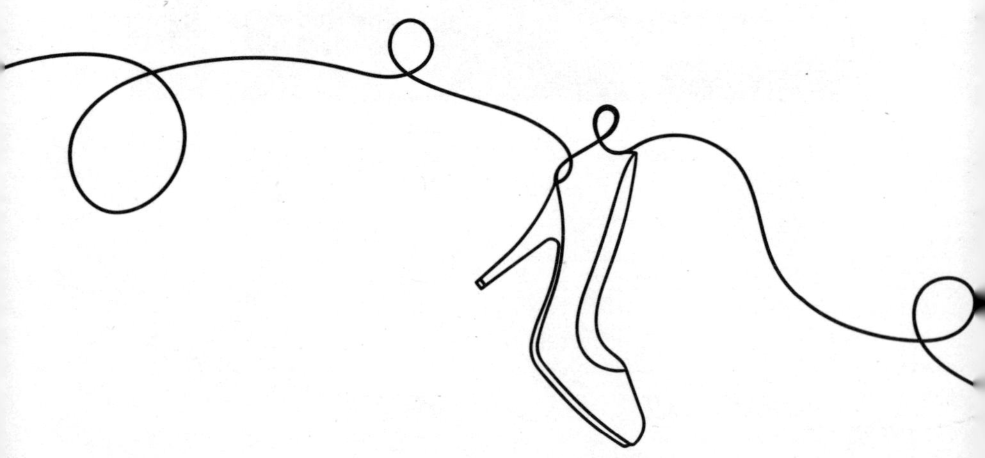

~ 103 ~

MATCH

Match the celebrity to their dance partner.

1. Angela Rippon
2. Sam Quek
3. Bobby Brazier
4. Krishnan Guru-Murthy
5. Gemma Atkinson
6. Toyah Willcox
7. Tom Fletcher
8. Annabel Croft
9. Hamza Yassin
10. Wynne Evans

a) Neil Jones
b) Johannes Radebe
c) Kai Widdrington
d) Aljaž Škorjanec
e) Katya Jones
f) Lauren Oakley
g) Nikita Kuzmin
h) Jowita Przystał
i) Dianne Buswell
j) Amy Dowden

~ 104 ~

A PERPLEXING POSER

What is suggested by the following?

DALATNCE

~ 105 ~

CRYPTOGRAM

Solve the cryptogram to discover what Shirley Ballas likes about the start of each series of *Strictly*. To give you a start, D = K, R = W, S = B and Z = H.

F	'G		Y	A	A	D	F	T	B
	'					K			

N	A	C	R	X	C	P		I	A		X
			W								

Y	F	I	I	Y	J		S	F	I		A	N
							B					

E	Q	X	C	D	Y	J		A	T		I	Z	A	E	J
				K								H			

P	X	C	D		R	F	T	I	J	C
			K		W					

T	F	B	Z	I	E
			H		

~ *106* ~

MINI SUDOKU

With their humour, knowledge, feedback and those all-important scores, the judges are an essential part of *Strictly*, and they also play a key role in this puzzle. Complete the grid so that every row, column and 2 x 3 box contains the letters that make up the word 'judges'.

G					J
				E	U
S			E		
	D				
J			D	S	

~ *107* ~

ANAGRAMS

Unscramble the following to reveal things either featured in, or with connections to, *Strictly*.

1. Battle grill
2. OK, taste wit
3. Graced upon
4. Now chased
5. Broader deal

~ 108 ~

WORD SEARCH

At some time, celebrities and their partners have danced to all the following. Find them in the grid and the unused letters will spell out another song used on *Strictly*. What is this?

Bamboleo	Fever	Lost	Tattoo
Big Spender	Hello Dolly	Open Arms	Two Hearts
Cherish	Hero	Perfect	Uptown Girl
Fashion	Hung Up	Poison	Wings

R	E	D	N	E	P	S	G	I	B	N
W	T	O	P	E	N	A	R	M	S	O
H	S	I	R	E	H	C	A	P	L	I
K	O	I	N	E	F	E	V	E	R	H
G	L	T	W	O	H	E	A	R	T	S
H	U	N	G	U	P	O	N	F	S	A
O	O	T	T	A	T	U	N	E	S	F
B	A	M	B	O	L	E	O	C	H	I
N	L	R	I	G	N	W	O	T	P	U
H	E	L	L	O	D	O	L	L	Y	E
N	O	S	I	O	P	S	G	N	I	W

~ *109* ~

A-MAZE-ING

The Glitterball is both sparkling and a-maze-ing, and this maze gives you the chance to work your way from the outside to its sparkly centre.

~ 110 ~

DOMINOES

Rearrange the dominoes to reveal words and names connected with *Strictly*. As an example, when the following dominoes are rearranged, the words Salsa and Tango appear.

A	S	L	A	S
A	G	N	O	T

S	A	L	S	A
T	A	N	G	O

1. Rearrange the following dominoes to reveal two winners of *Strictly*. Who are they?

L	I	B	B	I	A	L	Y	L	E
I	L	E	E	E	L	A	H	L	C

2. Rearrange the dominoes to reveal two words sometimes heard on *Strictly*. What are they?

S	S	D	T	R	A	I	E
B	L	F	O	S	U	A	U

~ *111* ~

CROSS OUT

Cross out all the letters that appear more than once. The letters that are left, reading from top to bottom and left to right, will spell out an important element of *Strictly*. What is it?

D	L	P	F	Q	G	B	V
H	K	W	O	Y	E	N	J
R	V	G	D	T	Z	P	X
N	B	M	K	A	Q	F	L
X	O	E	U	H	J	S	W
G	A	Z	T	I	R	Y	C

~ 112 ~

FOLLOW THE LEADER

The names of three professional dancers have been entered in the grid below. The individual letters in each of the three names appear in the right order when the grid is followed anti-clockwise, but the names have been mixed together. Starting from the N, bottom right, discover who they are.

C	L	O	N	I	T	E
C						A
J		S	U	L		I
O		A		E		N
Y				O		V
P	O	X	P	N		N

~ 113 ~

WORD BUILDER

The letters spelling out something very central to *Strictly* have been numbered one to nine. Solve the clues to discover what it is.

Letters 6, 4, 3 and 9 mean to depend on

Letters 1, 7, 8 and 4 mean to refer to

Letters 4, 3, 7, 8 and 2 give us a select group

Letters 1, 4, 3, 2, 6 and 9 give us a salad vegetable

Letters 5, 2, 3 and 8 give us a waist band

1	2	3	4	5	6	7	8	9

~ 114 ~

STRICTLY WORD SEARCH

Find all the following words in the grid:

Ballroom
Blackpool
Celebrities
Cha Cha Cha
Charleston
Choreography
Clauditorium
Costume
Dance-off
Foxtrot
Glitterball
Glitz
Jive
Judges
Latin
Leaderboard
Lindy Hop
Music
Orchestra
Paddles
Paso Doble
Quickstep
Rumba
Salsa
Samba
Singers
Strictly
Tango
Voting
Waltz

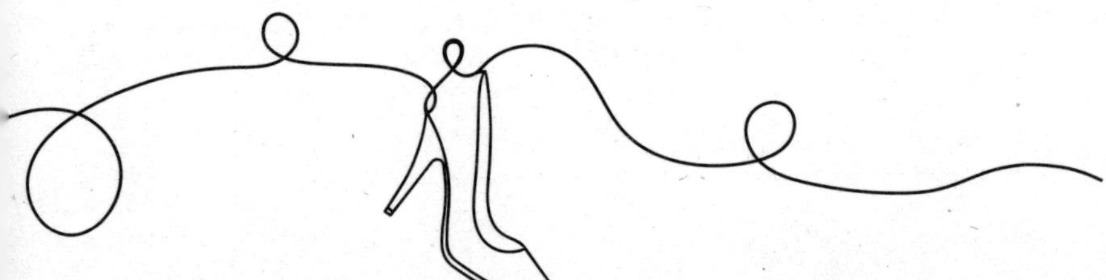

Q G Y C S R E G N I S O T O G G Z
C U S S E P A S O D O B L E H Q T
B K Y K C L A U D I T O R I U M L
L L L A B R E T T I L G S A M B A
A I E F A F A B D A N C E O F F W
T N V V L C H A R L E S T O N V E
I D I L L S A Q U I C K S T E P Z
N Y J O R E X R G V T Z J U M T E
I H J O O L B J T N L I S G S O M
O O S P O D K U P S I Y E N O R U
Z P T K M D B D A A E T W S K T S
G T R C T A N G O Z B H O X V X I
A O I A L P U E K X I M C V Z O C
S N C L V C O S T U M E U R K F I
L M T B G Y H P A R G O E R O H C
A I L F C H A C H A C H A M Z T J
S D Y L E A D E R B O A R D B X G

~ 115 ~

CROSSED WORDS

Using each of the letters provided in the grid, fill in the squares to form terms often heard on *Strictly*, with one part reading across and the other downwards. In the example below, the letters in the grid can be inserted in the squares to make 'Head Judge'.

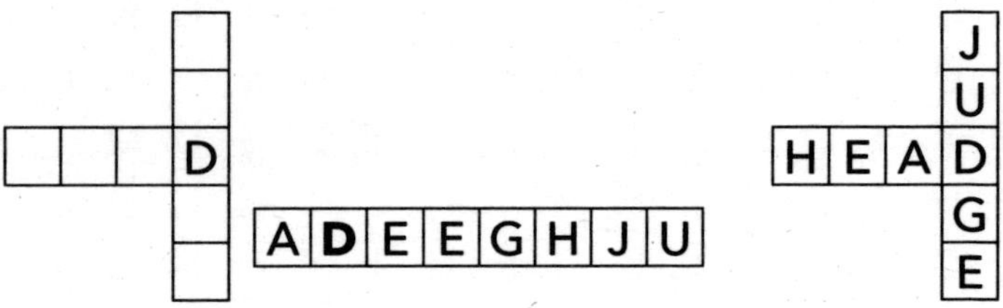

1.

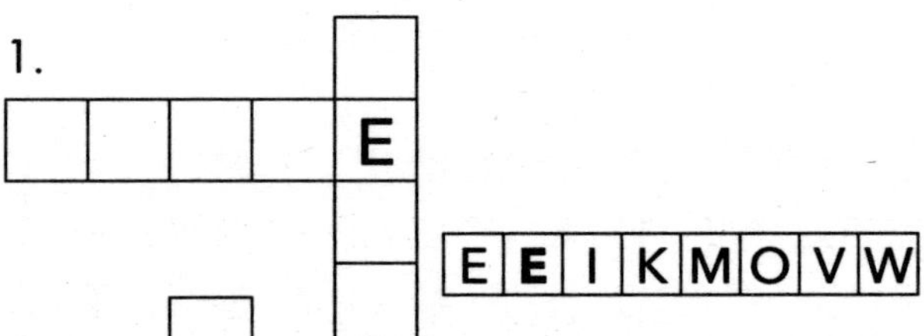

2.

~ 116 ~

HIDDEN WORDS

Which dances and dance steps are hidden in the following sentences? As an example, in the sentence, 'In Fiji very many enjoy dance,' the hidden dance is Jive (Fi**ji ve**ry).

1. What the professionals decided is completely different from the opening dance that was originally planned.
2. The designers were concerned about fake tan going over and staining some of the costumes.
3. Craig was particularly keen to watch as several celebrities now tried more ambitious routines.
4. Anton did well at indicating what he was looking for from the celebrities. They all rose to the challenge.
5. The judges were very interested in watching Sam. Ballroom dancing was obviously her forte.

~ 117 ~

TAKE YOUR PICK

1. What did Sarah Hadland practise in advance before appearing on *Strictly*?
    a) Getting used to wearing dancing shoes.
    b) Her Craig reaction face and how to look when he passed comment.
    c) Standing on one leg 'to improve my balance. I call it "my ostrich pose".'

2. What put a stop to Mark Ramprakash's salsa?
    a) His microphone got caught in his partner's dress.
    b) The necklace that Mark's partner was wearing broke, with lots of beads falling on the dance floor. After these had been quickly swept up, the couple were allowed to restart the routine.
    c) There was a temporary blackout in the studio.

3. Who were the 100th *Strictly* couple to dance in the Blackpool ballroom?
    a) Jamie Borthwick and Michelle Tsiakkas.
    b) Chris McCausland and Dianne Buswell.
    c) Montell Douglas and Johannes Radebe.

~ 118 ~

NAME TRACK

Find the starting letter. Then, moving one letter at a time – either horizontally, vertically or diagonally – discover the name of a celebrity who found the *Strictly* experience *'exhilarating'* – even *'a little terrifying'*, but went on to do very well in the competition. Who is the mystery celebrity?

A	R	C	L
O	N	E	B
F	T	N	A

~ *119* ~

DOWN THE MIDDLE

Each of the following words is missing a letter. Fill in the missing letter and you will find something in the shaded squares that is much anticipated. What is it?

T	A		E	S
G	R		N	D
R	I		E	R
I	D		A	L
B	A		O	N
S	T		L	E
M	O		S	E
M	A		C	H

~ 120 ~

WORD LADDER

When learning routines, celebrities have to consider their arm and leg movement. Similarly, in this word ladder, you too have to give consideration to arm and leg, as you change one letter at a time to turn the word 'arm' into 'leg'.

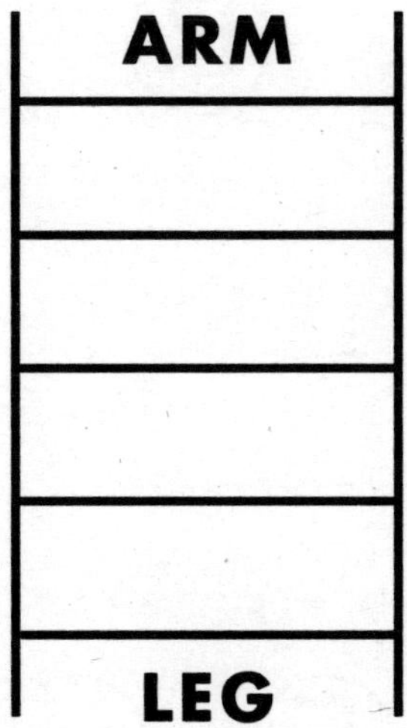

~ 121 ~

STAR NAME

The letters of the name of a *Strictly* star have been spread evenly around the circle. Find the first letter of this person's name and follow the letters in order to make up the star – and the star's name. Who is it?

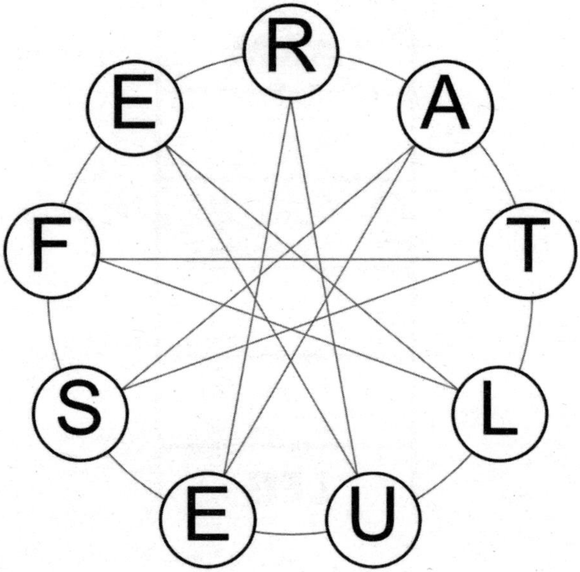

~ 122 ~

CRYPTOGRAM

Solve the cryptogram to reveal what Chris McCausland said about having Dianne Buswell as his dance partner. To give you a start, L = B, X = V and E = W.

A	G	C	■	H	A
			■		

Z	L	A	N	T	P	D	C	T	Q
	B								

N	X	C	S	■	D	G	C	■	B	N	N	I
	V			■				■				

G	Z	X	H	I	J	■	B	C
		V				■		

L	C	U	Z	P	A	C	■	A	G	C
B							■			

S	C	Z	T	T	Q	■	E	Z	I	D	A
						■	W				

I	N	X	C	B	L	C	S	■	N	K	K
		V			B			■			

~ 123 ~

CRISS-CROSS

All the following celebrities graced the *Strictly* dance floor some time ago, each of them bringing their own contribution and sparkle to the show. Find a place for them all in the grid.

7 LETTER NAME

Jamelia

8 LETTER NAMES

Danny Mac
Jake Wood

9 LETTER NAMES

Alex Scott
Anastacia
Anita Rani
Clara Amfo
Daisy Lowe
Jerry Hall
Lisa Riley

10 LETTER NAMES

Dani Harmer
JJ Chalmers
Nicky Byrne

11 LETTER NAMES

Anita Dobson
Helen George
Patsy Kensit
Scott Maslen
Tom Fletcher

12 LETTER NAMES

Holly Valance
Kellie Bright

13 LETTER NAMES

Chelsee Healey

Natalie Gumede

14 LETTER NAMES

Greg Rutherford

Steve Backshall

16 LETTER NAME

Pamela Stephenson

17 LETTER NAME

Sophie Ellis-Bextor

~ 124 ~

LETTER DROP

The letters in each of the columns need to be entered into the squares directly below, but not necessarily in the same order. By placing the letters in the correct squares, you will discover an interesting observation from Claudia Winkleman and something very true.

							L						
				R	T	E	R		C	H			
		C	O	O	P	W	D	E	R	R	I		
		P	A	I	P	C	A	A	D	I	G		
	T	S	T	M	N	N	E	T	T	M	B	L	G
I	H	E	E	O	A	L	W	L	I	N	Y	N	Y
		'	■										
■	■											■	■
■	■	■	■	■				■	■	■	■	■	■
■						-							
■	■	■			■						■	■	■
■	■							■				■	■

~ *125* ~

MINI SUDOKU

Whether the celebrities or the audience are keen to know the result, that anticipation is always an exciting part of *Strictly*. This mini sudoku will give you a chance to ponder this important aspect by completing the grid so that every row, column and 2 x 3 box contains the letters that make up the word 'result'.

L		E	S		
E	S		L		
R	U				T
			R		

~ 126 ~

ANAGRAMS

Unscramble the anagrams to reveal the names of some of *Strictly*'s professional dancers.

1. Join 'n' else
2. We'd do many
3. Auk ran here
4. A cool top VIP
5. Enjoy a task

~ *127* ~

ON TRACK

Find the starting letter. Then, moving one letter at a time – either horizontally, vertically or diagonally – discover something that becomes very important to dancers while on *Strictly*. The answer is two words but what is it?

R	O	T	M
G	N	O	R
N	I	I	A

~ *128* ~

WORD SEARCH

Find all the following professional dancers in the grid and the unused letters will spell out some other important contributors to *Strictly*. Who are they?

Aljaž	Kai	Nancy
Amy	Karen	Neil
Carlos	Katya	Nikita
Dianne	Lauren	Vito
Jowita	Luba	

O	S	L	Z	A	J	L	A
I	T	N	A	O	K	B	K
Y	K	I	W	U	U	A	D
M	A	I	V	L	R	N	I
A	T	G	E	E	R	E	A
A	Y	C	N	A	N	I	N
C	A	R	L	O	S	L	N
S	A	T	I	K	I	N	E

~ 129 ~

A PERPLEXING POSER

What is suggested by the following?

NRUT

~ 130 ~

CROSS OUT

Cross out all the letters that appear more than once. The remaining letters, reading from top to bottom and left to right, will spell out something central to *Strictly*. What is it?

F	L	V	M	S	B	P	G
R	I	W	Y	Z	U	J	X
K	B	T	G	F	H	O	W
P	D	U	R	V	M	I	Q
J	Q	L	A	K	S	N	Y
O	H	C	X	E	G	Z	T

~ 131 ~

MATCH

Match the celebrity to their dance partner.

1. Angela Scanlon	a) Nancy Xu
2. Nick Knowles	b) Gorka Márquez
3. Sarah Hadland	c) Anton Du Beke
4. Layton Williams	d) Karen Hauer
5. Dr Punam Krishan	e) Luba Mushtuk
6. Jamie Laing	f) Carlos Gu
7. Joe McFadden	g) Nikita Kuzmin
8. Katie Derham	h) Johannes Radebe
9. John Whaite	i) Katya Jones
10. Will Mellor	j) Vito Coppola

~ 132 ~

MYSTERY WORD

Enter the following words into the grid so that another word appears in the diagonal shaded squares: this is often seen and enjoyed on the *Strictly* dance floor. What is it?

Circle	Glitzy
Dances	Swivel
Energy	Timing

<table>
<tr><td></td><td></td><td></td><td></td><td></td><td></td></tr>
<tr><td></td><td></td><td>I</td><td></td><td></td><td></td></tr>
<tr><td></td><td></td><td>I</td><td></td><td></td><td></td></tr>
<tr><td></td><td></td><td></td><td></td><td></td><td>Y</td></tr>
<tr><td></td><td></td><td></td><td>C</td><td></td><td></td></tr>
<tr><td></td><td></td><td></td><td>C</td><td></td><td></td></tr>
</table>

~ 133 ~

WHAT MOTSI SAID

The following quotes have some of Motsi Mabuse's words missing. What did Motsi actually say?

1. In talking about what makes a Strictly champion: *'I think it's a combination of beautiful dancing, a great personality, chemistry and …'*

   a) sharing the journey with the audience.
   b) improving each week.
   c) immersing yourself in the *Strictly* experience.

2. In giving advice to the celebrities, Motsi said: *'Work hard on the ____ – it always pays off in the end.'*

   a) footwork
   b) fundamentals
   c) technique

3. As for what Motsi wants to see from the contestants: *'I want to see the celebrities giving 100 per cent. It's about …'*

   a) commitment.
   b) being in the moment.
   c) energy.

~ 134 ~

A RIDDLE

My first is in twist but not in turn,

My second is in teach, never in learn.

My third is in dance but not in style

While my fourth is in grin, never in smile.

My fifth is in lights, not in glow,

And my dazzling whole makes up a big part of the show.

What or who am I?

~ *135* ~

WORD LADDER

The celebrities learn much from the feedback of judges, and here's a chance to enjoy some positive feedback yourself, as you change, one letter at a time, the word 'feed' into 'back'.

FEED

BACK

~ 136 ~

CELEBRITY MIX

The names of five *Strictly* celebrities have been split and placed on random jigsaw puzzle pieces. Match the letters below to discover who they are.

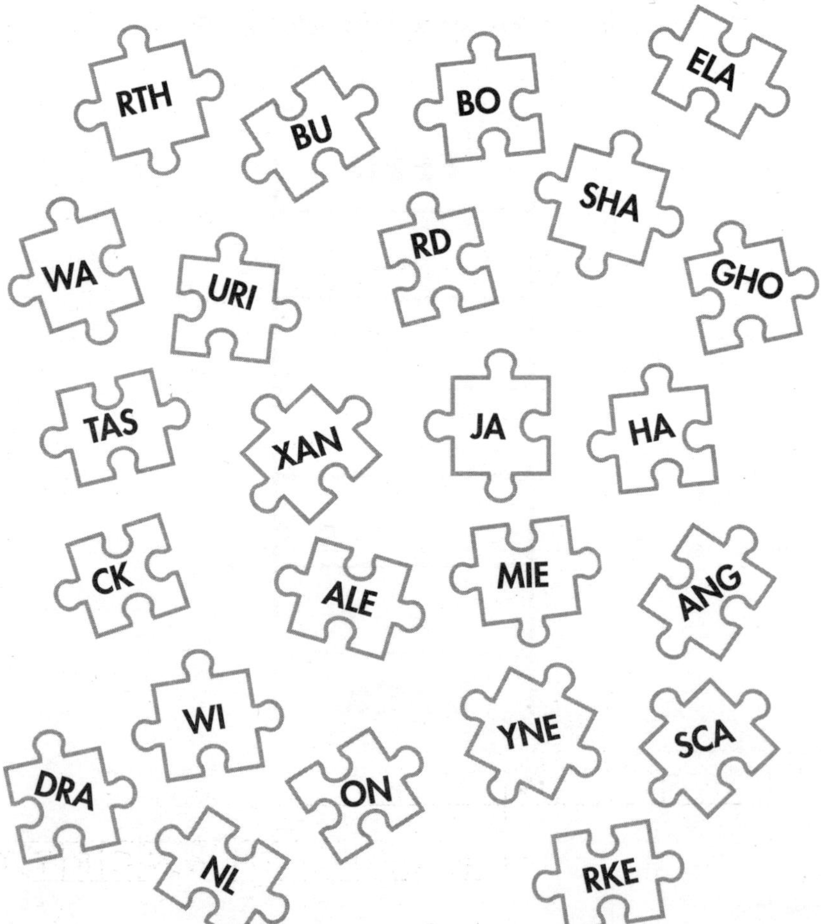

~ 137 ~

CROSSED WORDS

Using each of the letters provided in the grid, fill in the squares to form terms often heard on *Strictly*, with one part reading across and the other downwards. In the example below, the letters in the grid can be inserted in the squares to make 'Head Judge'.

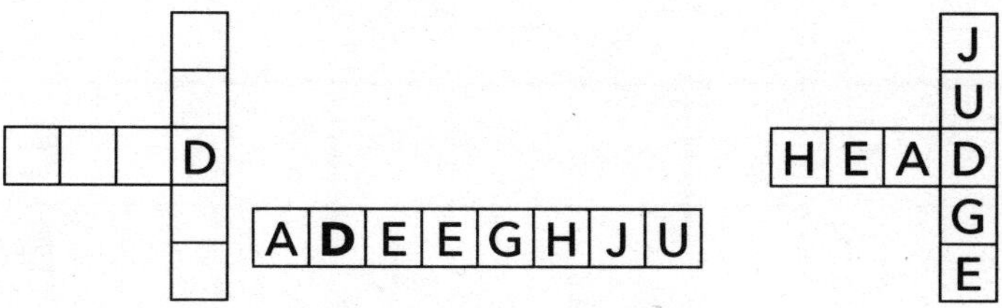

1.

2.

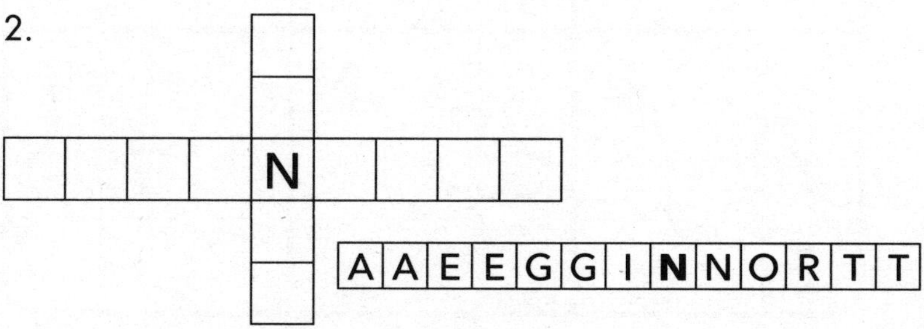

~ 138 ~

MYSTERY SUDOKU

Complete the grid so that every row, column and 3 x 3 box contains the letters EIJNORTUY in some order. One row or column contains a seven-letter word which celebrities often speak about while on *Strictly*. What is the mystery word?

	R							E
	U				I			R
T			N			I		
J					E			
	E	T		J		U	O	
			T					J
		E			N			I
Y			O				T	
I							J	

~ 139 ~

MYSTERY STARS

Some letters have been removed from the names of some *Strictly* celebrities and replaced with an asterisk. Who are the mystery stars?

1. **S*A **O*R*
2. *H*Y*E *A*D
3. **L*E *E*C*
4. *E*E *I*K*
5. *A*A* *AD*A*D
6. *A**A *A*S*N

~ 140 ~

TAKE YOUR PICK

1. Which *Strictly* winner was the first ever to perform a bare-chested Showdance?

    a) Louis Smith
    b) Tom Chambers
    c) Chris Hollins

2. The Cucaracha is a classic dance step seen on *Strictly* but, when literally translated, what does Cucaracha mean?

    a) caterpillar
    b) crab
    c) cockroach

3. Ellie Leach and Vito Coppola agreed that if they reached the final, they would get a matching tattoo, which they did. It was of a bee – but with what as its body?

    a) a 10 paddle
    b) an aubergine
    c) the Glitterball

~ 141 ~

WORD SEARCH

Find all the following words in the grid and the remaining letters will reveal the name of a dancing step. In which two dances is this step commonly seen?

Botafogo	Enchufla	Lift	Turn
Chassé	Fleckerl	Ronde	Volta
Cucaracha	Gancho	Spin	Weave

C	N	O	E	V	A	E	W	E
U	A	G	N	R	U	T	W	F
C	L	O	N	I	P	S	G	L
A	F	F	R	Y	T	E	A	E
R	U	A	O	V	F	S	N	C
A	H	T	N	O	I	S	C	K
C	C	O	D	L	L	A	H	E
H	N	B	E	T	O	H	O	R
A	E	R	K	A	E	C	R	L

~ *142* ~

ON THE RIGHT TRACK

Starting with the circled letter and moving one letter at a time, either horizontally, vertically or diagonally, discover something used on *Strictly* which helps reduce the environmental impact of the series. The answer is two words.

<table>
<tr><td>(B)</td><td>R</td><td>O</td><td>R</td><td>G</td></tr>
<tr><td>E</td><td>I</td><td>D</td><td>E</td><td>A</td></tr>
<tr><td>T</td><td>T</td><td>E</td><td>B</td><td>D</td></tr>
<tr><td>I</td><td>L</td><td>G</td><td>L</td><td>A</td></tr>
</table>

~ *143* ~

STAR NAME

The letters of the name of a *Strictly* star have been spread evenly around the circle. Find the first letter of this person's name and follow the letters in order to make up the star – and the star's name. Who is it?

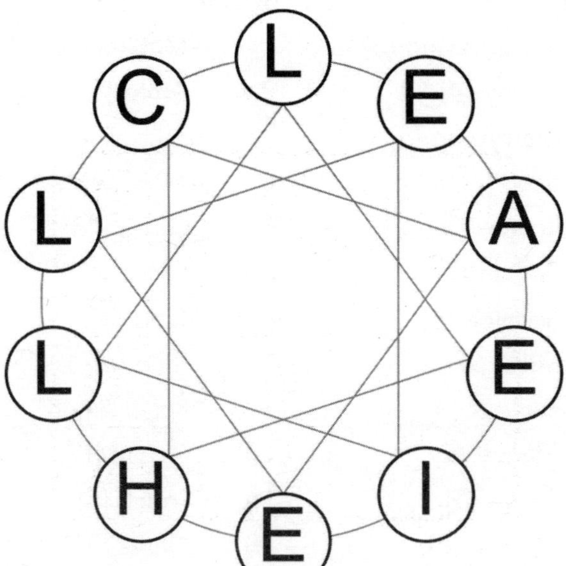

~ 144 ~

CROSSWORD: ON FIRST NAME TERMS

The answers are all the first names of the following *Strictly* celebrities.

ACROSS

2. __ McCausland (5)
4. __ Cundy (4)
6. __ Merrygold (5)
9. __ Scott (4)
10. __ Ravens (3)
12. __ Benton (4)
13. __ Scanlon (6)
14. __ Mills (5)
16. __ Willcox (5)
17. __ Clancy (5)
20. __ Andre (5)
22. __ McGee (6)
23. __ Bastian (3)
24. __ Skelton (5)

DOWN

1. __ McGuiness (3)
2. __ Amfo (5)
3. __ McFadden (3)
4. __ Murray (4)
5. __ Gough (6)
7. __ Oduba (3)
8. __ Judd (5)
10. __ Vine (6)
11. __ Kaplinsky (7)
12. __ Goss (4)
15. __ Leach (5)
18. __ Conley (5)
19. __ Kadi (5)
20. __ Merson (4)
21. __ Ayling-Ellis (4)

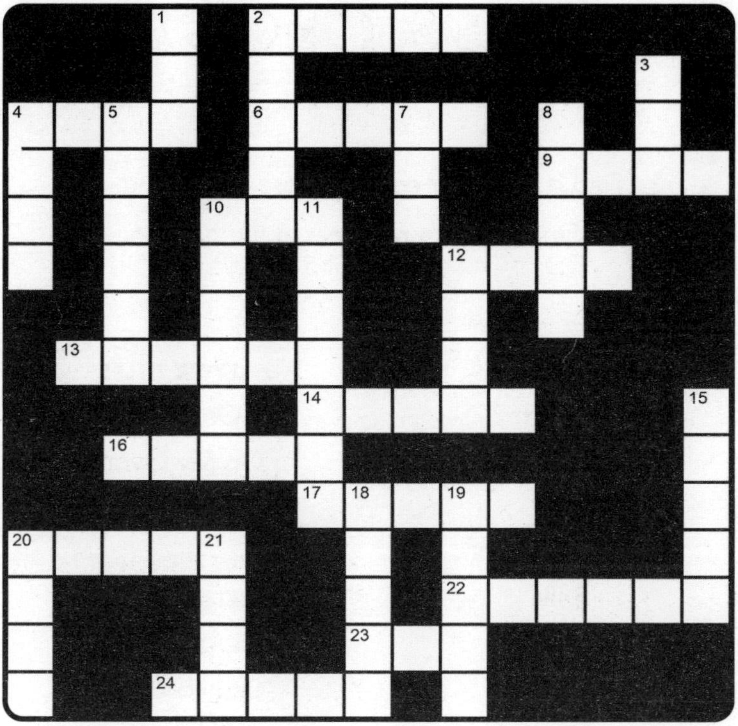

~145~

CRISS-CROSS

Find a place for each of these songs and *Strictly* dance numbers in the grid.

4 LETTER TITLES

Cuba
Iris

5 LETTER TITLES

Belle
Faith
Fever
Giant
Samba

6 LETTER TITLES

Butter
Golden
My Girl
Tattoo

7 LETTER TITLES

Get Busy
On My Own
Perfect

8 LETTER TITLES

Baby Face
Bamboleo
Believer
Dynamite
Jealousy

9 LETTER TITLES

End of Time
Last Dance
Two Hearts

10 LETTER TITLE

Uptown Girl

11 LETTER TITLES

Fascination

True Colours

12 LETTER TITLES

Magic Moments

This Ole House

13 LETTER TITLES

I love to Boogie

Sweet Caroline

~ 146 ~

CRYPTOGRAM

In thinking about what makes a winner, Motsi Mabuse said, '*Winners have a certain spark*' and, she added, a combination of what? To discover what this winning combination is, solve the cryptogram. To give you a start, E = P, R = B, G = W and L = U.

E	C	Y	Y	F	Q	P,
P						,

V	X	V	F	W	C	B	F	Q	P	■	C	P	V
										■			

B	J	X	■	C	R	F	O	F	B	K	■	B	Q
			■		B						■		

W	Q	P	P	X	W	B	■	G	F	B	J
							■	W			

B	J	X	■	C	L	V	F	X	P	W	X
			■		U						

~ 147 ~

DOMINOES

Rearrange the dominoes to reveal words connected with *Strictly*. As an example, when the following dominoes are rearranged, the words Salsa and Tango appear.

A	S	L	A	S
A	G	N	O	T

S	A	L	S	A
T	A	N	G	O

1. Rearrange the dominoes to reveal two things often seen on *Strictly*.

L	T	R	G	A	I	E	L	L	B	T
R	D	B	L	A	A	R	D	E	O	E

2. Rearrange the dominoes to reveal two things that feature on *Strictly*.

I	A	S	S	T	A	C	R	E
I	A	M	N	U	S	I	C	S

~ *148* ~

A-MAZE-ING

Here's a chance to take to the floor and dance your way to the centre with a few twists, turns – and maybe a few reverse turns – on the way.

~ 149 ~

PROPS WORD SEARCH

Over the years the *Strictly* Props department has sourced, as well as created, many wonders. In this word search, there is the word 'Props' to source and find. Where is the elusive 'Props?'

P	S	R	P	R	P	O	S	P	S	R
O	P	R	O	O	R	P	S	P	O	R
S	S	O	P	O	P	S	O	P	O	P
P	S	R	R	O	P	S	O	P	S	R
O	S	R	P	R	R	S	R	O	P	O
S	P	O	R	O	S	O	P	P	S	S
S	R	R	S	O	P	S	R	O	P	O
S	P	R	R	S	O	R	P	R	S	P
S	R	P	O	P	O	S	P	S	R	P
O	P	R	R	P	O	R	S	O	S	O
R	O	S	R	O	P	S	O	P	R	S

~ *150* ~

CROSS OUT

Cross out all the letters that appear more than once. The remaining letters, reading from top to bottom and left to right, will spell out something often seen and enjoyed on *Strictly*. What is it?

H	P	K	C	Y	I	S	G
T	N	F	Q	G	O	E	V
D	X	W	P	L	T	J	R
G	C	E	V	K	F	Z	Q
J	Z	U	X	N	M	L	H
S	B	W	O	I	A	D	Y

~ 151 ~

TRIVIA

1. What animal appeared at the end of Bill Bailey's Dr Doolittle routine?
2. Which drummer struck up a winning beat in *Strictly* series 9?
3. At the start of Movie Week in series 22, Shirley Ballas did not appear with the other judges until she gracefully descended on the stage holding a parasol and dressed as which character?
4. In which year did Anton du Beke become a permanent judge on *Strictly*?
5. To date, who has been the oldest celebrity to take part in *Strictly*?
6. In the 2024 *Strictly Come Dancing* Christmas Show Josh Widdicombe dressed up as what sort of bird?
7. Who has been the lead singer on *Strictly* since the show began?

~ 152 ~

WORD LINK

Each of the three word groups in the clues below has a word in common. For example, if the clues were 'spirit', 'crossing' and 'best', the answer would be 'level' ('spirit level', 'level crossing' and 'level best'). Answer each of the following clues correctly and something that is often used on *Strictly* will be revealed. What is it?

1. home, alone, behind
2. fair, safe, group
3. wedding, mix, shop
4. secret, still, going
5. start, lunch, arrive
6. thing, miss, enough
7. dance, big, together

1			
2			
3			
4			
5			
6			
7			

~ 153 ~

LETTER DROP

The letters in each of the columns need to be entered into the squares directly below, but not necessarily in the same order. By placing the letters in the correct squares, you will discover why Craig Revel Horwood was 'very disappointed' after watching Ali Bastian and partner Brian Fortuna perform the Viennese Waltz in Blackpool Week.

			C		T				N			
	I		D	N	U		S	R	T	O	L	
	I	H	W	I	G	H	D	I	N	G	G	
F	T	N	I	O	A	L	W	I	O	N	T	E
■		■						■				■
				■		■						
■						■						■
■	■	■					■			■	■	■

~ 154 ~

WORD SEARCH

Find all the following words in the grid. When you have found them all, in the remaining squares you will discover what Angela Rippon thinks *Strictly* is *'on every level'*.

Dance	Music	Tango
Glitz	Party	Trophy
Jive	Routine	Vote
Judges	Rumba	Waltz
Latin	Strictly	

R	V	Y	H	P	O	R	T	P
S	O	U	L	M	R	U	E	G
E	T	U	A	U	N	M	Y	L
Z	E	R	T	S	T	B	T	I
D	T	E	I	I	R	A	R	T
A	E	L	N	C	N	T	A	Z
N	V	A	A	G	T	E	P	I
C	I	N	O	W	M	L	E	N
E	J	U	D	G	E	S	Y	T

~ 155 ~

MYSTERY SUDOKU

Complete the grid so that every row, column and 3 x 3 box contains the letters ADEHILNOT in some order. One row or column contains a seven-letter word that is often seen and experienced on *Strictly*. What is the mystery word?

						T	L	
			L		I			D
T				O		I		E
A	N			E				T
	E			D			O	
I				N			H	L
D		O		A				I
E			T		O			
	I	N						

~ 156 ~

TAKE YOUR PICK

1. When Sarah Hadland went to the training room for the first time, what did she bring with her?
   a) Two bottles of carbonated water. 'I need to keep myself hydrated and I like a bit of fizz.'
   b) A bunch of bananas for energy.
   c) Teabags and kettle 'for a good brew'.

2. In week 5 of series 22 Shirley Ballas complimented JB Gill on ticking the boxes and said there are a lot of boxes to tick in dancing. She mentioned the personality box and the timing box, but what was the third box she mentioned?
   a) The musicality box.
   b) The posture box.
   c) The partnership-skill box.

3. In week 4 of series 22 Pete Wicks and his dancing partner Jowita Przystał danced a Quickstep with the backdrop of a tattoo parlour. At the end of the routine Pete was tattooed, but with what?
   a) A Glitterball.
   b) A picture of Craig Revel Horwood holding a 10 paddle.
   c) A silhouette of Pete and Jowita doing a jive.

~ 157 ~

FITTING WORDS

Fit the following words into the grid so that another word is created in the shaded squares. This is something seen and mentioned on *Strictly*. What is it?

Dancer	Music
Disaster	Partner
Lifts	*Strictly*
Movement	Twist

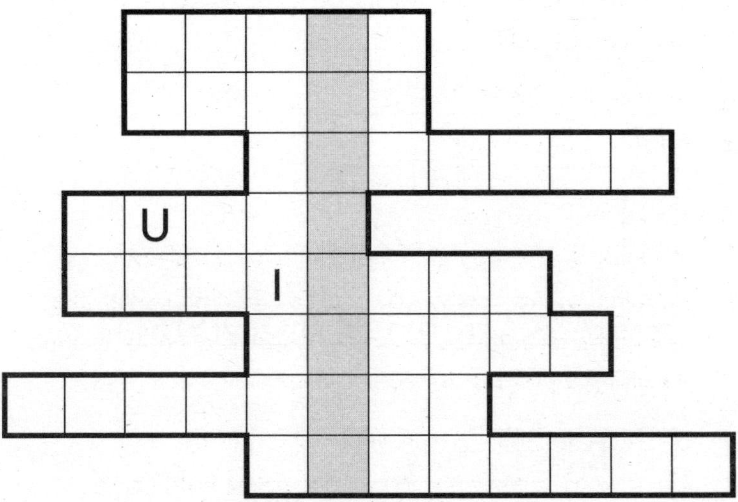

~ *158* ~

CROSSED WORDS

Using each of the letters provided in the grid, fill in the squares to form terms often heard on *Strictly*, with one part reading across and the other downwards. In the example below, the letters in the grid can be inserted in the squares to make 'Head Judge'.

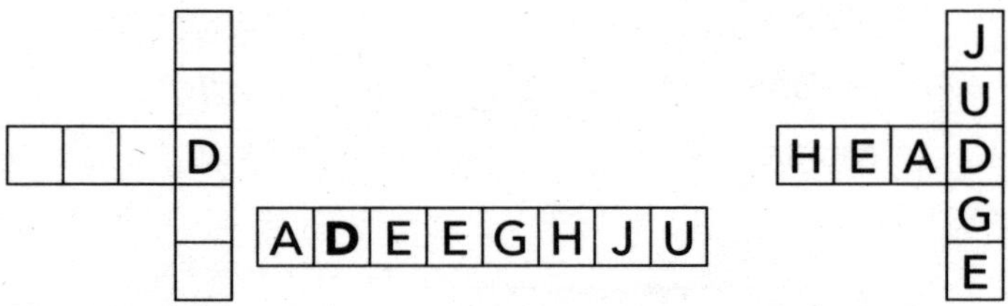

1.

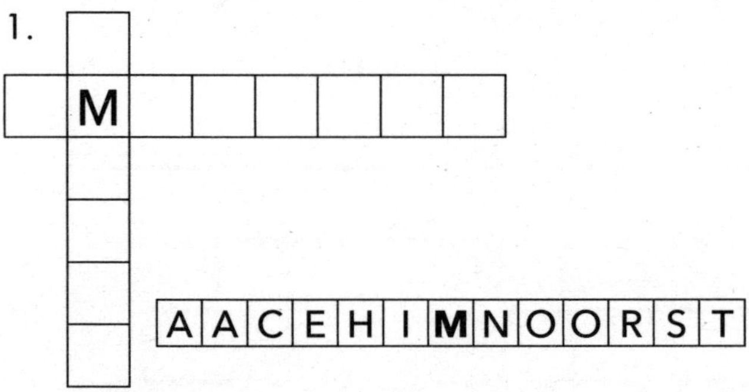

2.

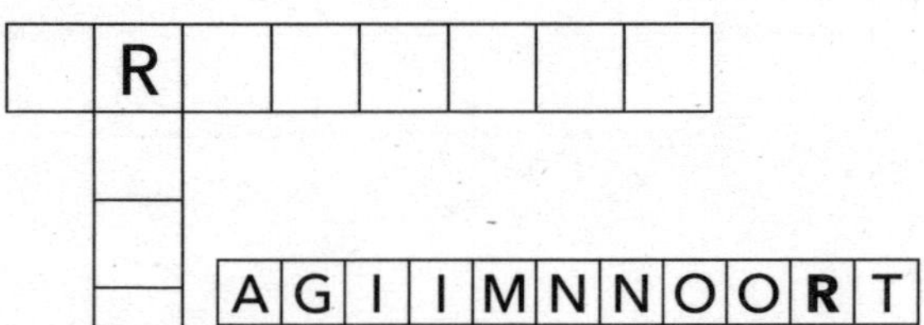

~ 159 ~

CELEBRITY MIX

The names of five *Strictly* celebrities have been split and placed on random jigsaw puzzle pieces. Match the letters below to discover who they are.

~ 160 ~

WORD LADDER

Whether following in the footsteps of other celebrities or making sure they do not get a foot step wrong, here's a chance to consider footstep in more detail as you change, one letter at a time, the word 'foot' into 'step'.

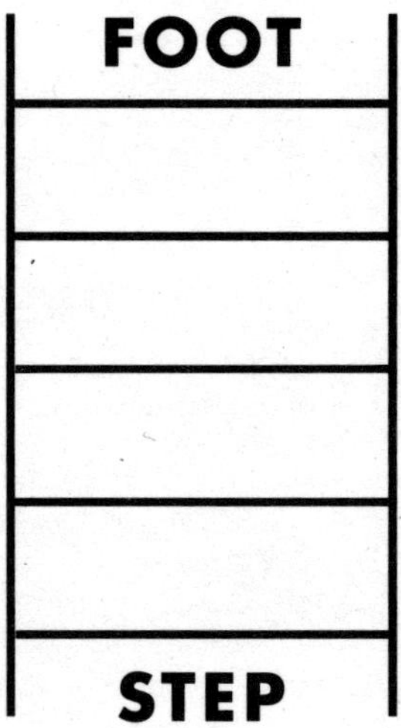

~ 161 ~

STAR NAME

The letters of the name of someone well-known to *Strictly* fans have been spread evenly around the circle. Find the first letter of this person's name and follow the letters in order to make up the star – and the star's name. Who is it?

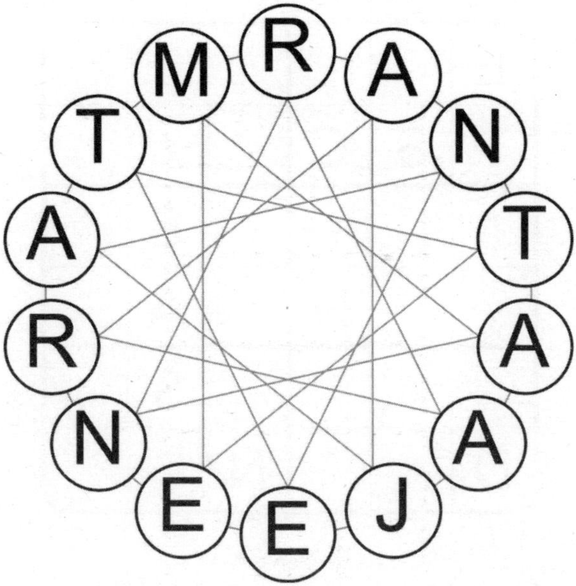

~ 162 ~

MINI SUDOKU

Strictly is a celebration of dance, with each show containing a good mix of different dances. Complete the grid so that every row, column and 2 x 3 box contains the letters that make up the word 'dances'.

E					
	S	C			
				E	
		N		A	
				S	
D			N		

~ *163* ~

WORD CIRCLES

Each circle of letters makes up a word relating to *Strictly*. The letters are written in either a clockwise or anti-clockwise direction. Can you identify the words?

1\.
I
N N
G I
T A
R

2\.
D
I U
E A
N E
C

3\.
A
B F
U S
L U
O

4\.
C
T A
I R
C P
E

5\.
A
P E
P S
L U
A

6\.
I
C R
T T
L S
Y

~ *164* ~

WHAT THEY SAID

The following quotes have some of their words missing. What did the following actually say?

1. Tess Daly believes the recipe for success in *Strictly* is hard work and commitment. *'My advice is to ...'*

   a) learn as much as you can from the professionals and judges. Take on board what they say.
   b) bring your heart to the dance floor, because the more you give, the more we will love you for it.
   c) throw yourself into the competition and have fun. It's an amazing experience.

2. Janette Manrara said, *'Every year, the celebrity line-up ...'*

   a) takes us on an incredible journey.
   b) brings something fresh and different to the dance floor.
   c) surprises us with their talent.

3. Talking at the start of series 21, Shirley Ballas said, *'Whatever people may lack in dance experience, they'll certainly make up for ...'*

   a) in their willingness to give it a go.
   b) in the fun they will have.
   c) in larger-than-life personalities.

~ 165 ~

FOLLOW THE LEADER

The names of three people who have played or play a big part in *Strictly* have been entered in the grid below. The individual letters in each of the three names appear in the right order when the grid is followed anti-clockwise, but the names have been mixed together. Starting from the T, bottom right, discover who they are.

D	E	M	S	V	A	S
Z						A
A		H	I	S		H
A		N		Y		E
L				S		D
A	Y	R	A	C		T

~ 166 ~

GLITTERBALL WORD SEARCH

In every series the celebrities work hard to get their hands on the Glitterball trophy. It can be elusive, but in this word search there is a chance for you to secure the famed Glitterball. Where is it in the grid?

G B T
R E L B G I E
T B I E B I L T A A A
R L E L I T G R A G E R E
T I A I G L A E T A T G T T E
E I T L B R G T A L L E G T B
T R G R L T A T L L E B G L R T E
R B L T B A T L G R G R L I G B L
A T E G R L I R I T B A B I T B T L R
L G I B T T E T G L R G A T L R G L G
A T R L B B G R T R L E B T T G L A E
B L E G L T A G E I R A E B B E L
A I A T G G R T B A L G R G R L A
L E G L E B R I L I A B B I L
T B E G G R G A A B B A T A L
A L G B L T E L R L L R E
R L E G B G T A L L R
I G T A L L E
R E T

~ *167* ~

DANCING TARGET

Just as celebrities set themselves a target with their own dances, this puzzle offers a dancing target of a different sort. Make as many words of three or more letters out of 'dancing' as you can. No names allowed.

DANCING

16+ words – fab-u-lous

11–14 words – well done

3–10 words – good. Worthy of a 7 paddle!

0–2 words – dis-ah-ster

~ *168* ~

CHRISTMAS WORD SEARCH

All the following were Christmas champions in *Strictly* Christmas Specials. Each has a special place in the tree, but where are they?

Anne-Marie
Aston Merrygold
Debbie McGee
Jamie Borthwick
JB Gill
Katie Derham
Louis Smith
Tayce

```
            M
          Y A A
          G H S
        U J R T U
        X D E O Z
      C K E D N H X
      G I B E M T E
    G V O B I E I A P
    F Q F I T R M I Q
  Z D Y X E A R S O E D
  P T S B M K Y S G C H
  L Q V E C T G I J Y Z
C A L N Y G V O U C A H X
P J N I N E F L O L T I J
Y A J N G E C D L M F F V
Y J A M I E B O R T H W I C K
            J
        U N I A R
        P E G M J
        Y P G L P
        R I J I Z
```

~ *169* ~

MYSTERY SUDOKU

Complete the grid so that every row, column and 3 x 3 box contains the letters ACDEINRTV in some order. One row or column contains a seven-letter word connected with the judges, as well as being important to all involved on *Strictly*. What is the mystery word?

			D		C			
	I							E
	N			R	T			D
E		C		N		D	T	
	T	D		E		A		N
R			I	D			A	
N							I	
			C		N			

~ *170* ~

A PERPLEXING POSER

What is suggested by the following?

The answer is two words.

L L L L L

D

O O O O O

~ 171 ~

WORD LADDER

To avoid injury, it is always important for dancers to warm up and then cool down. Here is a chance to follow suit and, in this word ladder, change one letter at a time to go from 'warm' to 'cool'. If you manage it, hot stuff!

WARM

COOL

~ 172 ~

TRIVIA

1. What was introduced in series 5 and, except for series 8 and 9, has become a major feature of the *Strictly* competition?
2. Which dance on *Strictly* shares its name with a city in South Carolina?
3. What is the catchphrase Tess and Claudia say at the end of each show?
4. The Cucaracha is a classic step in which dance?
5. How long is the average *Strictly* routine?
6. What is Anton Du Beke's favourite dance, which he described as *'a proper dance. It has class'*?
7. What new themed week was introduced in series 22?

~ 173 ~

CRYPTOGRAM

Solve the cryptogram to discover what Hamza Yassin said after his win on *Strictly*. To give you a start, B = V, S = F, Y = W, A = J and I = B.

P		G	D	B	M		S	D	U	U	M	K
				V			F					

P	K		U	F	B	M		Y	P	H	G
					V			W			

V	D	K	E	M		D	K	V		H	G	M

A	F	N		P	H		I	W	P	K	L	Z
J							B					

H	F		J	M	F	J	U	M	'Z
									'

S	D	E	M	Z
F				

~ *174* ~

FITTING WORDS

Fit the following words into the grid so that a word often heard on *Strictly* is created in the shaded squares. What is it?

Heel	Rumba	Spin
Lifts	Samba	Tango
Routine	Smooth	Waltz

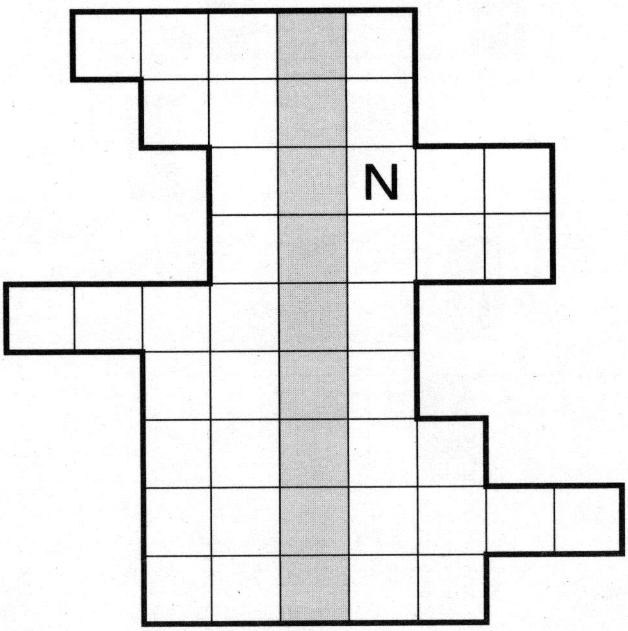

~ 175 ~

MATCH

Match the celebrity to their professional dance partner.

1. Stacey Dooley	a) Katya Jones
2. Joe Sugg	b) Amy Dowden
3. Ed Balls	c) Janette Manrara
4. Adam Thomas	d) Johannes Radebe
5. Molly Rainford	e) Kai Widdrington
6. James Bye	f) Carlos Gu
7. Montell Douglas	g) Vito Coppola
8. HRVY	h) Kevin Clifton
9. AJ Odudu	i) Luba Mushtuk
10. Fleur East	j) Dianne Buswell

~ 176 ~

CODEWORD

Each letter of the alphabet has been replaced by a number. To solve the puzzle, you must decide which letter is represented by which number. To help you start, one of the words has been partly filled in. When you have solved the code, complete the bottom grid to discover a special nickname earned by which judge?

1	2	3	4	5	6 I	7	8	9	10	11	12	13
14	15	16	17	18	19	20	21	22	23 A	24 R	25	26

18	17	5	5	7	■	8	15	■	19	23	26	6	7

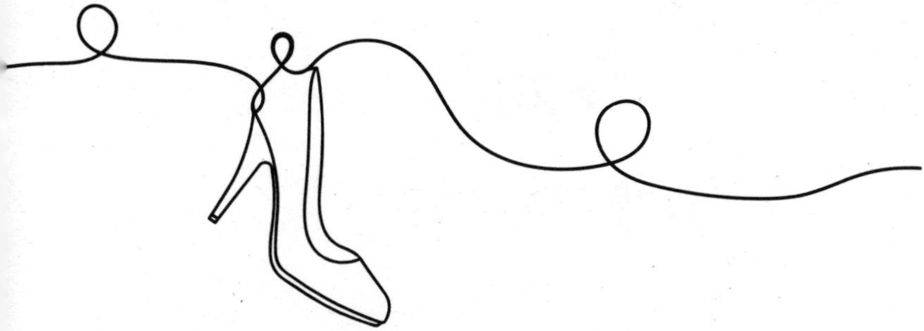

■	24	■	10	■	6	■	3	■	17	■	5	■	11	■
24	5	13	23	6	7	■	23	11	11	5	7	16	6	9
■	21	■	21	■	22	■	21	■	16	■	10	■	10	■
3	23	13	5	2	20	4	5	■	23	10	14	6	7	12
■	19	■	24	■	19	■	19	■	26	■	17	■	6	■
18	17	23	7	12	8	■	6	7	5	15	15	5	10	26
■	5	■	■	■	26	■	7	■	■	■	19	■	■	■
23	16	16	24	5	2	2	■	5	16	20	23	19	19	2
■	■	■	5	■	■	■	10	■	8	■	■	■	5	■
26	5	2	2	16	23	19	4	■	25	8	13	20	23	26
■	9	■	5	■	20	■	11	■	7	■	6	■	15	■
5	10	19	23 A	6 I	24 R	■	24	5	2	5	13	20	19	5
■	6	■	26	■	17	■	5	■	6	■	6	■	5	■
23	26	26	5	13	11	26	2	■	1	5	7	6	26	14
■	5	■	16	■	26	■	2	■	5	■	12	■	2	■

~ 177 ~

A RIDDLE

My first is in samba but not in dance,

My second is in move, never in stance.

My third is in music but not in score,

My fourth is in less, never in more.

My fifth is in dance but not in hall,

My sixth is in lifts, never in fall.

And my cheery whole is so often seen

on the Strictly scene.

What am I?

~ *178* ~

MINI SUDOKU

With its glamour, glitz and excitement, *Strictly* is a success around the world, with the BBC licensing the format to over 60 countries. In this mini sudoku, help celebrate the *Strictly* format by completing the grid so that every row, column and 2 x 3 box contains the letters that make up the word 'format'.

	R		O		
					F
		T	A		
	M				
O					T
			R	O	

~ *179* ~

LETTER DROP

The letters in each of the columns need to be entered into the squares directly below, but not necessarily in the same order. By placing the letters in the correct squares, you will discover something Bill Bailey hoped his success on *Strictly* would show.

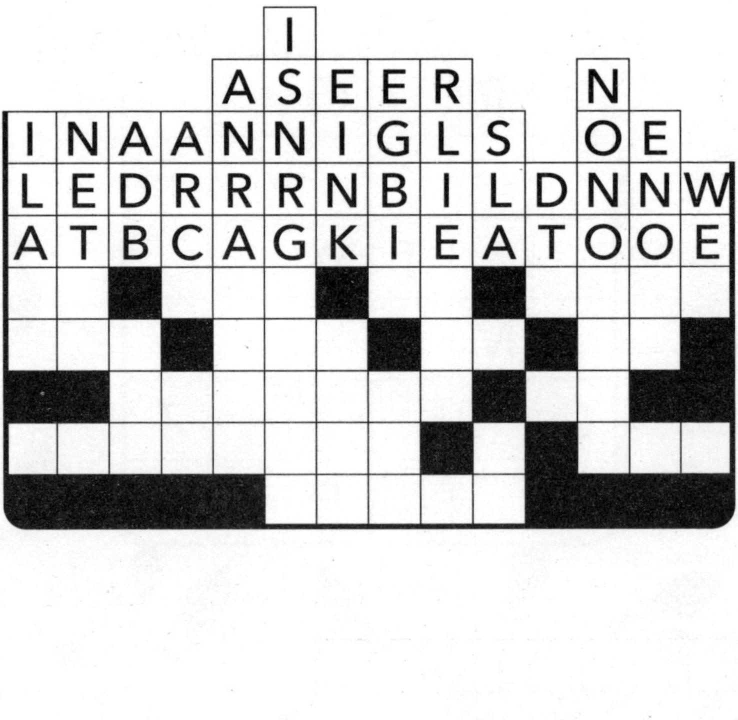

~ *180* ~

CROSSED WORDS

Using each of the letters provided in the grid, fill in the squares to form terms often heard on *Strictly*, with one part reading across and the other downwards. In the example below, the letters in the grid can be inserted in the squares to make 'Head Judge'.

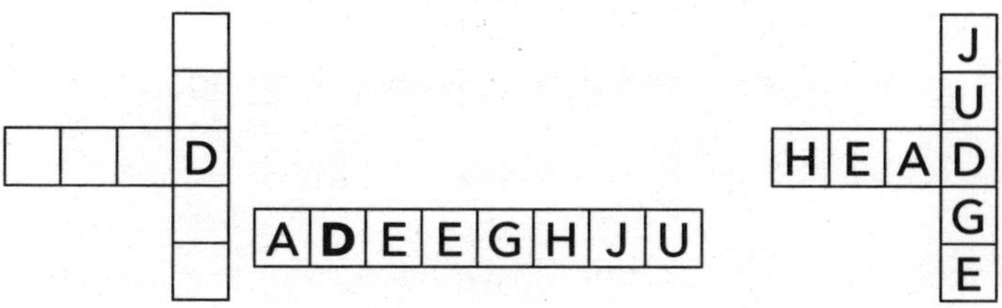

1.

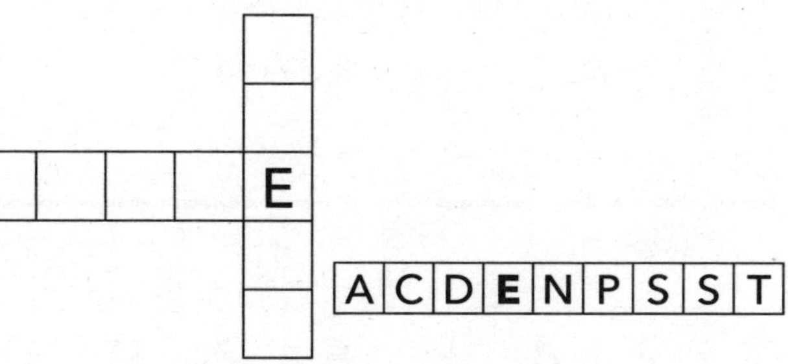

2.

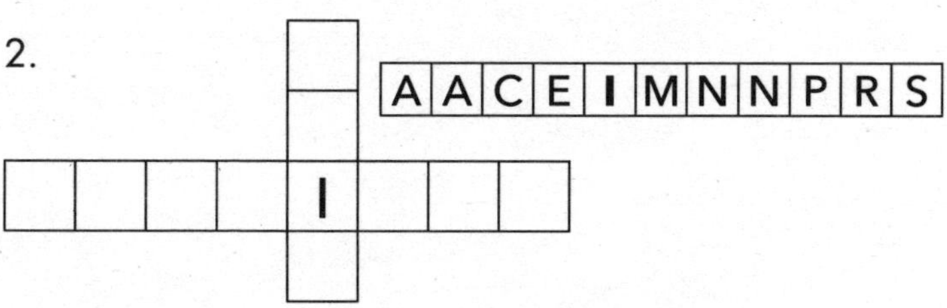

~ *181* ~

WORD BUILDER

The letters spelling out something the judges pay great attention to have been numbered one to nine. Solve the clues to discover what it is.

Letters 4, 6, 5 and 1 give us a clue

Letters 3, 8, 1 and 2 give us something adorable

Letters 3, 4, 6 and 5 give us a facial feature

Letters 3, 4, 9, 7, 8 and 2 give us a means of payment

Letters 7, 8, 6 and 1 cause us to give up
but hopefully not in this case

1	2	3	4	5	6	7	8	9

~ 182 ~

CROSS OUT

Cross out all the letters that appear more than once. The remaining letters, reading from top to bottom and left to right, will spell out something judges often refer to on *Strictly*. What is it?

C	H	L	B	P	N	G	V
U	D	O	K	S	X	J	Y
N	I	P	Z	T	H	Q	C
K	Q	G	U	B	L	D	X
O	C	F	J	V	I	R	N
T	A	Y	M	S	E	Z	P

~ 183 ~

WORD LADDER

Strictly is fun to watch and, as Motsi Mabuse said, *'People are looking for a good time.'* In this word ladder, you too will have a good time as you change, one letter at a time, the word 'good' into 'time'.

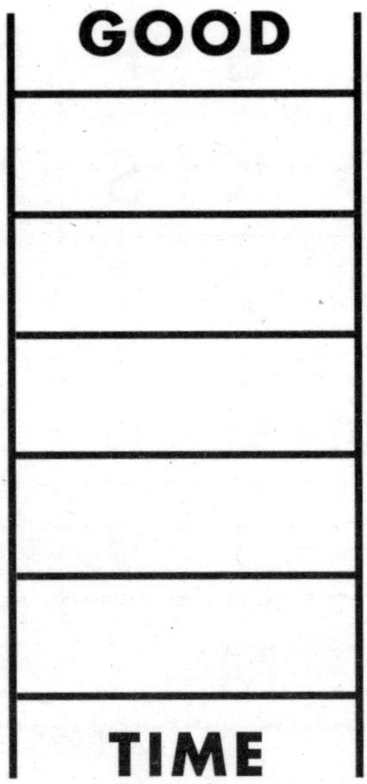

~ 184 ~

MYSTERY WORD

Fit each of the dances and dance terms into the grid so that another dancing term is created in the shaded squares. What does this term mean?

Salsa	Gancho
Samba	Musicality
Chaîné	New Yorker

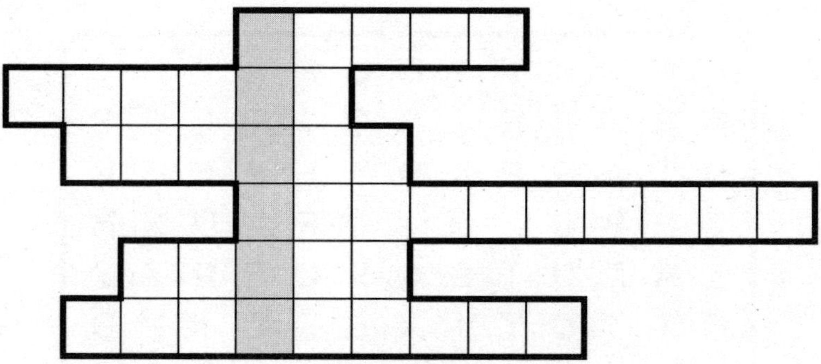

~ *185* ~

WORD SEARCH: THE P'S

In week 9 of series 22 Shirley Ballas told JB Gill to remember the 7 P's and then '*the sky would be the limit*'. The P's Shirley mentioned were: 'Practice and perseverance of postural principles promising physical perfection.'

Find these 7 words beginning with P in the grid below.

P D H S V P M Q P A Z Q I
H R O P R I N C I P L E S
D T A R P K D I E P F E P
Z P B C Y R I L P L D X H
L A R U T S O P Q E P Z Y
R T T C Y I X E R L I P S
H P P I E N C I P L P S I
E C N A R E V E S R E P C
P N O L P C E P R E P U A
T H P Z E E F X I L U P L
G L N O I T C E F R E P K
I P R P E K H P N F O I I
P E G N I S I M O R P R P

~ 186 ~

MATCH

Strictly has drawn on some of the best professional dancers from around the world to partner the celebrities. Match the dancer to their country of origin.

1. Karen Hauer
2. Gorka Márquez
3. Amy Dowden
4. Aljaž Škorjanec
5. Oti Mabuse
6. Nancy Xu
7. Jowita Przystał
8. Kai Widdrington

a) Wales
b) South Africa
c) China
d) England
e) Poland
f) Venezuela
g) Slovenia
h) Spain

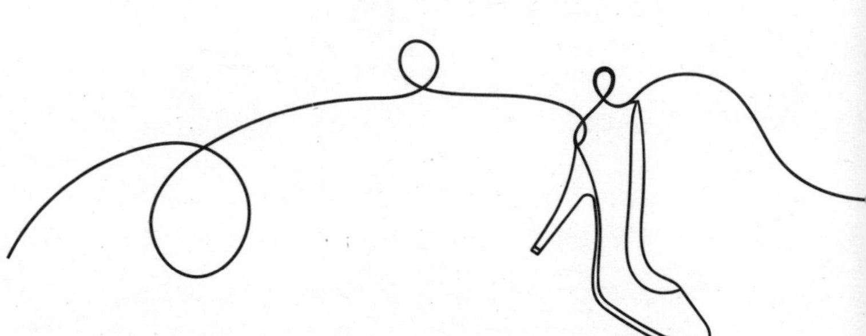

~ 187 ~

STAR NAME

The letters of the name of a *Strictly* star have been spread evenly around the circle. Find the first letter of this person's name and follow the letters in order to make up the star – and the star's name. Who is it?

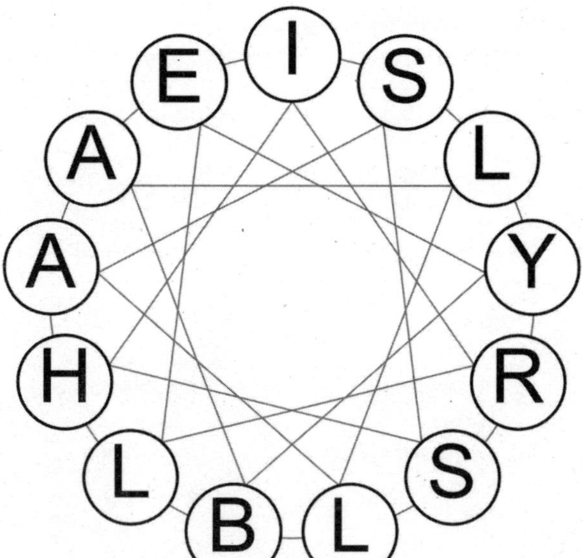

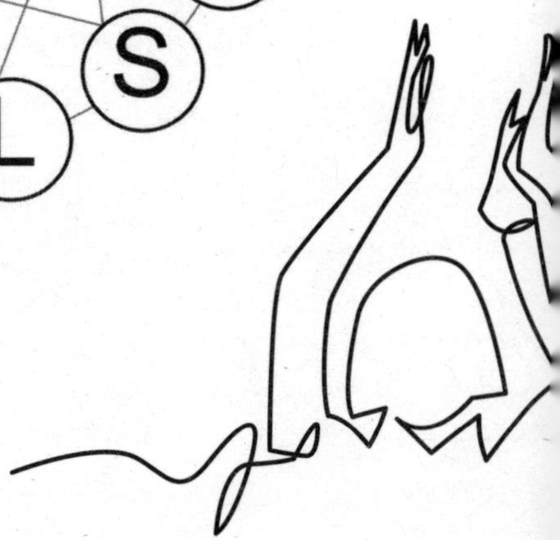

~ 188 ~

A *STRICTLY* CONUNDRUM

What is odd about this paragraph?

With its popularity, high standards, music, dancing, fashion, glitz, glamour, laughs and many highlights (including a hilarious Cha-cha-cha by Bill and Oti), many saw Saturday night's show. Full of laughs, it was a triumph and an obvious joy for all who took part. As Anton said, many will look forward to watching this particular *Strictly* again.

~ *189* ~

BETWEEN THE LINES

Something that is much anticipated on *Strictly* can be inserted in the middle line so that, reading downwards, nine three-letter words are formed. What is it?

A	W	C	A	A	O	A	I	T
P	Y	T	E	D	R	T	E	N

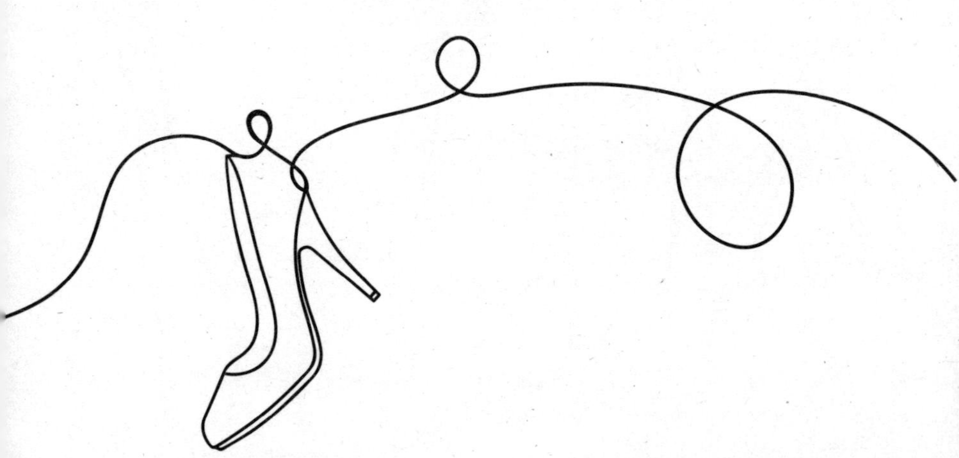

~ 190 ~

HIDDEN NAMES

The first name of a professional dancer is hidden in each of the following sentences. Who are they?

1. In the dance-off, they were especially slick, aiming to impress all four judges.
2. Tonight, the couple could have chosen to dance to a ballady-type song or karaoke style. They chose the latter.
3. Several celebrities, after a lot of hard work, are now back in contention.
4. She enjoyed dancing with a comedian, never expecting to win.
5. It was in the Quickstep they particularly shone. I'll be looking forward to hearing what the judges have to say.

~ 191 ~

MINI SUDOKU: TROPHY

In each series there is only one celebrity who gets to hold the famed Glitterball trophy but here is a chance to enjoy securing a trophy of your own by successfully completing the grid, so that every row, column and 2 x 3 box contains the letters that make up the word 'trophy'.

H				P	
	R		H		
		R	O		
P					
				Y	
			R		T

~ 192 ~

ANAGRAMS

Unscramble the following to discover the names of five professional dancers, including one who took part in many of the early series.

1. Make this ace skill
2. Ah, and serene job!
3. A joy – waltz trips
4. Adoring kind wit
5. Noble dancer

~ 193 ~

FITTING WORDS

Fit the following words into the grid so that another word is created in the shaded squares – it's something that celebrities hope to become.

Ballroom	Costume	Latin	Samba
Chassé	Fake tan	Music	Tempo

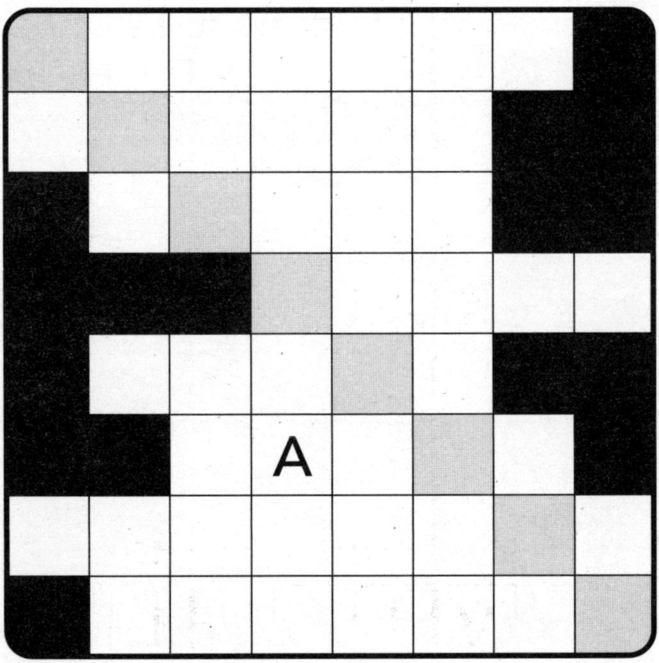

~ 194 ~

MYSTERY SUDOKU

Complete the grid so that every row, column and 3 x 3 box contains the letters AEILMRTVY in some order. One row or column contains a seven-letter word and something appreciated about *Strictly*. What is the mystery word?

<table>
<tr><td></td><td></td><td>I</td><td></td><td></td><td>V</td><td>R</td><td></td><td>L</td></tr>
<tr><td>E</td><td></td><td>L</td><td></td><td></td><td></td><td></td><td></td><td></td></tr>
<tr><td></td><td>T</td><td></td><td></td><td>M</td><td>R</td><td></td><td></td><td></td></tr>
<tr><td>T</td><td>Y</td><td></td><td></td><td></td><td></td><td></td><td></td><td></td></tr>
<tr><td>A</td><td></td><td>R</td><td></td><td></td><td></td><td>T</td><td></td><td>V</td></tr>
<tr><td></td><td></td><td></td><td></td><td></td><td></td><td></td><td>M</td><td>I</td></tr>
<tr><td></td><td></td><td></td><td>T</td><td>E</td><td></td><td></td><td>R</td><td></td></tr>
<tr><td></td><td></td><td></td><td></td><td></td><td></td><td>E</td><td></td><td>Y</td></tr>
<tr><td>Y</td><td></td><td>V</td><td>I</td><td></td><td></td><td>L</td><td></td><td></td></tr>
</table>

~ *195* ~

NAME TRACK

This celebrity said, *'At the start my main goal was not to go out first. But then I realised that the public really love a trier ...'* And this celebrity certainly tried and won huge support. To discover who they are, find the starting letter in the grid below. Then, moving one letter at a time – either horizontally, vertically or diagonally – reveal their name.

E	Y	S	Y
L	T	D	E
O	O	A	C

~ *196* ~

LETTER DROP

The letters in each of the columns need to be entered into the squares directly below, but not necessarily in the same order. By placing the letters in the correct squares, you will discover what Anton Du Beke hoped celebrities would say of their *Strictly* experience.

		A			A	
A	I	A		A	N	Y
T	H	T	T	V	E	D
A	M	G	Z	W	N	S
I	L	L	A	I	M	G
	■					■
				■		
			■			
■			■			

~ 197 ~

CROSS OUT

Cross out all the letters that appear more than once. The remaining letters, reading from top to bottom and left to right, will spell out something the *Strictly* judges recognise and like. What is it?

C	S	E	N	H	B	T	G
J	Q	D	U	O	P	W	K
V	Y	M	F	Z	C	X	M
K	W	N	S	G	V	L	J
H	A	X	C	U	Q	B	T
O	I	P	Z	D	R	E	Y

~ *198* ~

WORD TRACK

Find the starting letter. Then, moving one letter at a time – either horizontally, vertically or diagonally – discover a popular feature of *Strictly*.

I	T	R	C
D	O	L	I
U	A	M	U

~ *199* ~

A PERPLEXING POSER

What is suggested by the following?

E

K

A

M

~ 200 ~

CRYPTOGRAM

For the last puzzle, a *Strictly*-inspired haiku by Neil Somerville. To give you a start, K = W, X = V, Z = C and V = L.

C	Q	P	■	T	Q	I	K	■	Y	T
			■				W	■		

I	X	P	A,	■	T	G	R	A	W	V	Y	F	S
	V		,	■						L			

U	P	U	I	A	Y	P	T	■	A	P	U	R	Y	F.
								■						.

P	Z	Q	I	P	T	■	I	D
	C					■		

V	R	L	S	Q	C	P	A.
L							

ANSWERS

1. Anagrams

1) Paso Doble, 2) Charleston, 3) Argentine Tango, 4) American smooth, 5) Viennese Waltz

2. Cross Out

Jive

3. Mystery Sudoku

P	U	L	O	T	E	M	S	R
O	T	R	S	M	L	P	E	U
S	M	E	U	R	P	O	L	T
T	P	S	L	U	R	E	M	O
U	E	O	M	P	S	R	T	L
R	L	M	E	O	T	S	U	P
E	O	P	T	S	U	L	R	M
M	S	U	R	L	O	T	P	E
L	R	T	P	E	M	U	O	S

4. Trivia

1) 2004, 2) eight, 3) Jill Halfpenny, 4) walnuts, 5) Charleston, 6) Bollywood, 7) Viennese Waltz

5. Letter Drop

You have a hip action that could crack coconuts.

6. Criss-Cross

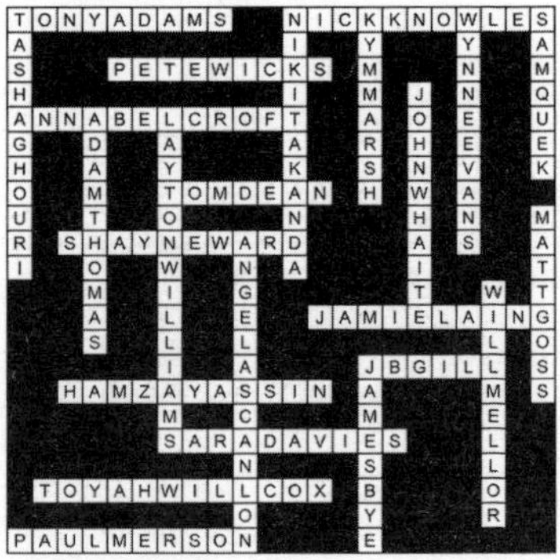

7. Word Search: Dance Terms

The hidden dance term is 'Cuban motion', a tricky hip action seen in Latin dances.

8. What They Said

1c, 2b, 3b

9. Word Ladder
Here is one possible solution: move, love, lose, lost, last, fast.

10. Follow the Leader
Carlos Gu, Amy Dowden, Karen Hauer

11. Cryptogram
Dance is about expressing yourself, being authentic and showing who you are.

12. Hidden Away
1) advise, 2) catchy, 3) indoor, 4) scores, 5) relish. The words reading downwards in the shaded squares, and which dancers need to 'choose' with great care, are 'dance shoes'.

13. Take Your Pick
1c, 2c, 3a

14. Word Builder
Paso Doble

15. Criss-Cross: Professional Dancers

16. Star Name
Tess Daly

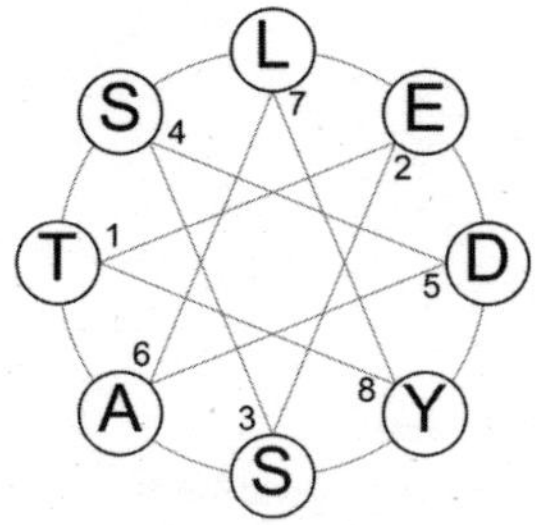

17. Word Link
1) pipe, 2) bear, 3) side, 4) code, 5) cold, 6) deep, 7) fast. The word in the shaded column is 'paddles'.

18. A Riddle
Humour

19. Word Track
Choreography

20. Word Search: Pioneers

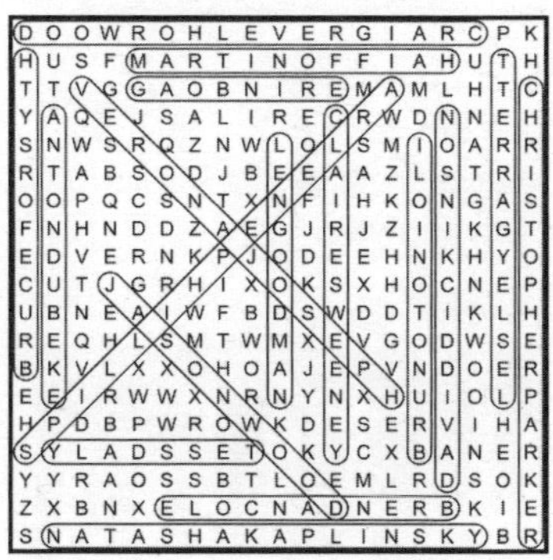

21. Mini Sudoku: Laughs

U	L	A	H	S	G
S	H	G	L	U	A
A	S	L	U	G	H
G	U	H	S	A	L
H	A	U	G	L	S
L	G	S	A	H	U

22. Word Ladder

Here is one possible solution: hand, band, bond, fond, food, foot

23. Mystery Sudoku

E	I	C	G	S	N	A	L	P
L	S	N	A	P	I	G	C	E
A	P	G	L	E	C	I	N	S
N	A	L	S	C	P	E	G	I
S	G	E	N	I	L	C	P	A
P	C	I	E	A	G	N	S	L
C	N	A	P	L	E	S	I	G
I	L	S	C	G	A	P	E	N
G	E	P	I	N	S	L	A	C

24. Celebrity Mix

Ellie Simmonds, Paul Merson, Maisie Smith, Molly Rainford, Nick Knowles

25. Criss-Cross

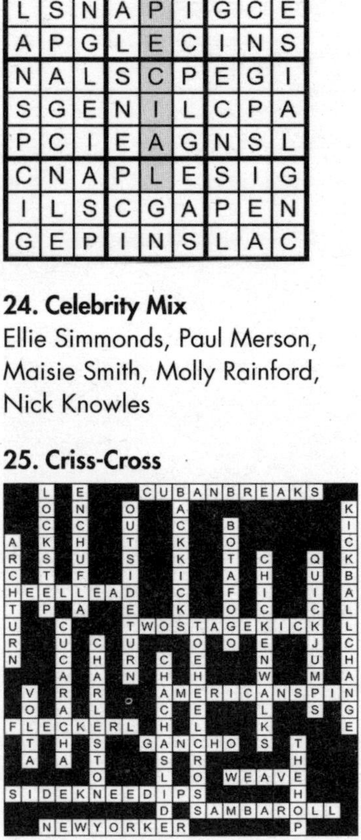

26. Letter Drop

They are the core and heartbeat of the show.

27. *Strictly* Conundrums

1) eight, 2) by standing back to back.

28. A-maze-ing

29. Cryptogram

Enjoy yourself and don't think about it as a competition.

30. Anagrams

1) Tess Daly, 2) Claudia Winkleman, 3) Craig Revel Horwood, 4) Shirley Ballas, 5) Motsi Mabuse

31. A Perplexing Poser

Sixteen. Well done if you included the 'd' in 'How many d's are on this page?'.

32. Cross Out

Waltz

33. Follow the Leader

JB Gill, Pete Wicks, Sarah Hadland

34. Word Search: Music

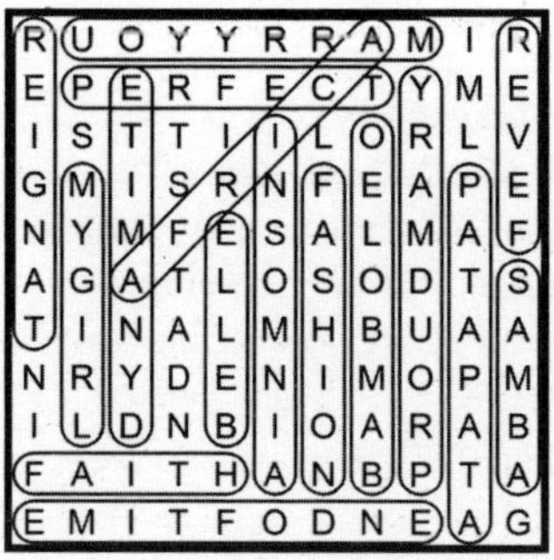

The hidden song was 'I'm Still Standing', written by Elton John and Bernie Taupin.

35. What They Said

1b, 2a, 3c

36. Name Track

Sarah Hadland

37. Dominoes

1) Group Dance, 2) Dave Arch, Tess Daly

38. Star Name

Bill Bailey, winner of the 2020 series of *Strictly*.

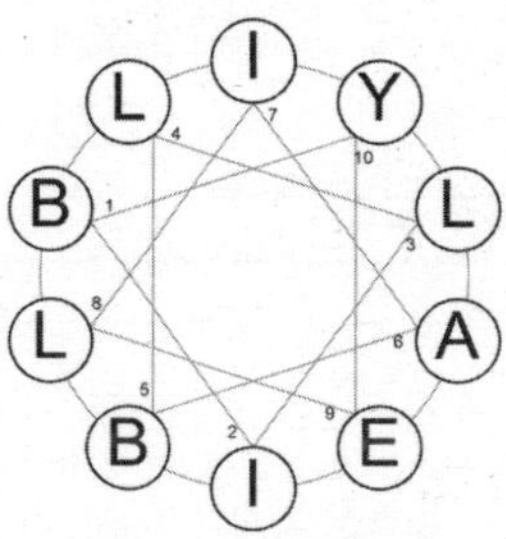

39. Hidden Words

1) Rumba, 2) Ronde, 3) Salsa, 4) Gancho, 5) Chaîné, 6) Feather Step

40. Mini Sudoku

A	T	N	E	R	B
B	E	R	A	N	T
N	A	E	B	T	R
T	R	B	N	A	E
R	B	A	T	E	N
E	N	T	R	B	A

41. Down Word

Anthem, season, palace, seesaw, random, Saturn. The shaded word is 'talent'.

42. Criss-Cross: Finalists

43. A Riddle

Poise

44. Match

1g, 2e, 3h, 4b, 5a, 6d, 7c, 8f

45. Codeword

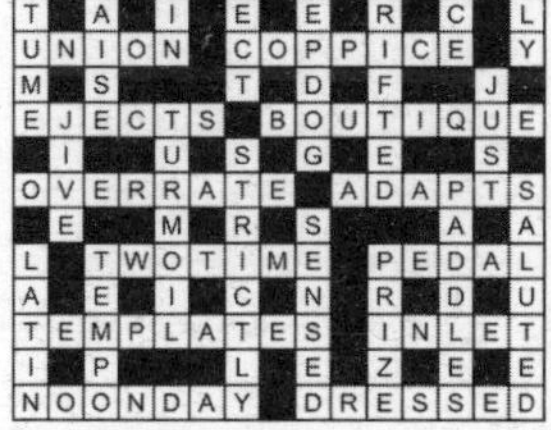

Tess Daly said, 'Our only agenda is joy.'

46. Anagrams
1) Ann Widdecombe, 2) Ed Balls, 3) Tony Adams, 4) Annabel Croft, 5) Ellie Simmonds

47. Word Search

Z	T	L	A	W	E	S	E	N	N	E	I	V	K	N
D	F	U	L	H	D	P	G	M	L	S	T	Z	M	J
J	B	M	P	T	N	N	O	B	S	R	A	P	C	A
M	V	R	M	O	W	Y	O	Z	C	G	A	L	F	J
B	H	X	V	O	V	D	Q	Y	N	B	Q	M	S	U
B	T	P	V	M	O	Y	F	I	M	Q	L	M	Y	A
E	V	I	J	S	G	M	F	A	U	S	N	T	S	G
B	L	D	A	N	X	T	S	I	K	L	O	X	A	G
Y	I	P	K	A	M	O	O	R	L	L	A	B	V	T
C	N	A	R	C	H	A	R	L	E	S	T	O	N	A
J	D	B	O	I	P	E	T	S	K	C	I	U	Q	N
X	Y	M	B	R	I	L	U	V	E	W	J	I	Y	G
K	H	U	R	E	W	T	O	R	T	X	O	F	W	O
R	O	R	C	M	L	C	H	A	C	H	A	C	H	A
T	P	I	N	A	Z	Y	N	X	Z	H	L	P	W	N

48. Crossed Words
1) Grand Final, 2) Couple's Choice

49. Celebrity Mix
Chris McCausland, Fleur East, Bobby Brazier, Toyah Willcox, Emma Bunton

50. Mystery Sudoku

H	P	O	S	R	L	A	E	K
A	L	S	P	E	K	H	O	R
E	K	R	A	H	O	S	P	L
P	O	K	R	A	H	E	L	S
L	E	H	K	P	S	R	A	O
R	S	A	L	O	E	P	K	H
O	H	L	E	S	P	K	R	A
S	A	E	O	K	R	L	H	P
K	R	P	H	L	A	O	S	E

51. Letter Drop
It just shows with opportunity and support and determination, anything can happen.

52. Down the Middle
Footwork

53. Take Away
1) Katie Derham, Anton Du Beke, 2) Bobby Brazier, Dianne Buswell, 3) Molly Rainford, Carlos Gu, 4) Joe McFadden, Katya Jones, 5) Tom Fletcher, Amy Dowden

54. Cryptogram
Ballroom is two people dancing together to music, touching in perfect harmony.

55. Taking the Lead
Sarah Hadland, Jamie Borthwick, Punam Krishan, Nick Knowles

56. Word Builder
Rehearsal

57. Special Feature
1) Charleston, 2) Elstree, 3) Hop, 4) Oduba, 5) Salsa, 6) New Yorker, 7) Dianne, 8) Argentine, 9) Waltz. When rearranged, the letters in the shaded squares spell 'Showdance'.

58. Word Search

S	L	T	I	S	R	C	T	R	I	L	C	T	I	Y
T	Y	R	T	Y	T	S	S	R	L	T	R	S	L	L
L	I	I	S	T	S	T	C	Y	L	I	S	I	Y	I
R	Y	R	C	T	L	R	Y	T	L	S	C	L	C	L
S	T	Y	I	R	C	T	Y	S	T	L	R	T	R	S
R	I	S	T	R	S	T	C	Y	S	Y	L	Y	C	Y
T	C	R	R	I	T	L	S	Y	R	I	L	S	R	I
R	L	Y	I	S	C	Y	T	S	L	C	L	Y	C	T
S	R	R	L	I	T	R	L	Y	I	Y	Y	S	C	R
T	T	S	R	C	I	R	R	Y	R	I	T	Y	I	T
I	C	T	Y	S	L	S	I	S	S	I	Y	L	T	S
R	Y	L	S	I	R	T	L	C	R	I	C	S	R	I
C	L	S	T	R	L	C	S	I	T	R	T	Y	Y	C
C	I	Y	C	L	I	T	C	T	I	L	S	C	Y	T
Y	L	S	T	I	C	S	T	R	Y	S	Y	I	Y	L

59. The A List
1) Adam Peaty, 2) Mark Ramprakash, 3) Danny Mac, 4) Sarah Hadland, 5) Hamza Yassin, 6) Ali Bastian, 7) Anastacia, 8) Shayne Ward, 9) Angela Scanlon, 10) Jayde Adams, 11) Dan Walker, 12) Clara Amfo

60. A Riddle
Energy

61. Name Track
Jay McGuiness, winner of the 2015 series of *Strictly*.

62. Crossword: On First Name Terms
ACROSS: 3) Greg, 5) Kelly, 6) Tyler, 7) Bobby, 11) Nigel, 12) James, 13) Wynne, 15) Hamza, 17) Andrew, 18) Martina, 19) Dev, 20) Molly, 23) Dan, 24) Matt, 25) Pete, 26) Sam.
DOWN: 1) Will, 2) Caroline, 3) Gabby, 4) Aled, 5) Kaye, 6) Tom, 8) Bill, 9) Cherie, 10) Punam, 12) John, 14) Layton, 16) Angela, 17) Adam, 21) Ore, 22) Les.

63. Cross Out
Makeup

64. Follow the Leader
Motsi Mabuse, Fleur East, Zoe Ball

65. Between the Lines
The something special is 'Halloween', which has often resulted in a spooktacular ballroom battle.

66. Mini Sudoku

L	R	I	W	T	S
W	S	T	R	I	L
T	L	W	S	R	I
S	I	R	L	W	T
I	W	L	T	S	R
R	T	S	I	L	W

67. Criss-Cross

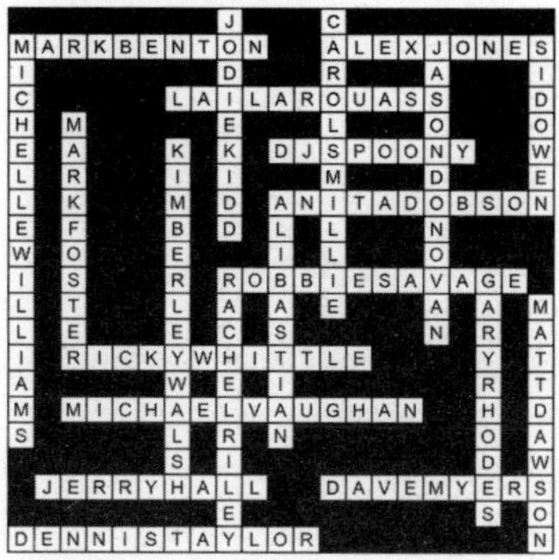

68. Word Ladder
Here is one possible solution: hip, hit, lit, let, leg

69. One from the Other
1) dance steps, 2) group dance, 3) arch turn, 4) heel lead, 5) Cuban walks

70. Sentence Gram
The marvellous work of the wardrobe department was very important in the rehearsal and the orchestra was also much involved in preparing for *Strictly Come Dancing*.

71. Word Link
1) made, 2) part, 3) open, 4) last, 5) lost. The word in the shaded column is 'dress'.

72. Star Name
Joe McFadden, winner of the 2017 series of *Strictly*.

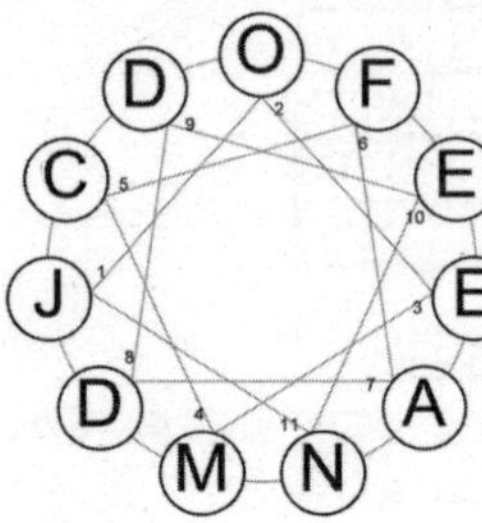

73. Take Your Pick
1b, 2c, 3b

74. Cryptogram
If you apply yourself you can actually improve as many people have done.

75. Cross Out
Style

76. A-maze-ing

77. Making an Entrance
1d, 2e, 3h, 4g, 5a, 6i, 7f, 8b, 9c

78. Letter Drop
Life is like a dance, with its own rhythm and tempo.

79. Word Ladder
Here is one possible solution: ball, bell, belt, bolt, boot, root, room

80. Word Search

Y	R	T	S	I	M	E	H	C
R	B	A	L	A	N	C	E	T
E	C	H	I	T	A	E	R	G
N	I	R	N	Y	D	O	B	K
T	S	L	O	O	U	T	D	S
R	U	I	E	O	D	E	O	T
A	M	H	E	G	L	B	O	O
P	S	M	R	A	S	F	G	X
G	N	I	D	N	U	O	R	G

Shirley was also looking for contestants who will 'think outside the box'.

81. Anagrams
1) Paul Merson, 2) Tom Dean, 3) Pete Wicks, 4) Nick Knowles, 5) Wynne Evans

82. Mystery Sudoku

M	A	I	G	H	U	O	R	L
G	O	R	L	I	M	A	H	U
H	L	U	A	O	R	G	M	I
L	G	A	M	R	H	I	U	O
U	I	H	O	A	G	M	L	R
R	M	O	U	L	I	H	A	G
I	U	G	R	M	A	L	O	H
O	H	M	I	U	L	R	G	A
A	R	L	H	G	O	U	I	M

83. Fitting Words
The words need to be inserted in the following order from top to bottom: *Strictly*, foxtrot, tango, music, routine, partner, ballroom. The word created in the shaded squares and something needed by all who take part in *Strictly* is 'stamina'.

84. Trivia
1) John Sergeant, 2) Salsa, 3) Natasha Kaplinsky, 4) 1920s, 5) Se-Ven, 6) A hooking action, 7) Couple's Choice.

85. Missing a Letter
Blackpool

86. Criss-Cross

87. Celebrity Mix
Stacey Dooley, Layton Williams, John Whaite, Montell Douglas, Debbie McGee

88. Cross Out
Lifts

89. Word Search: Celebrity

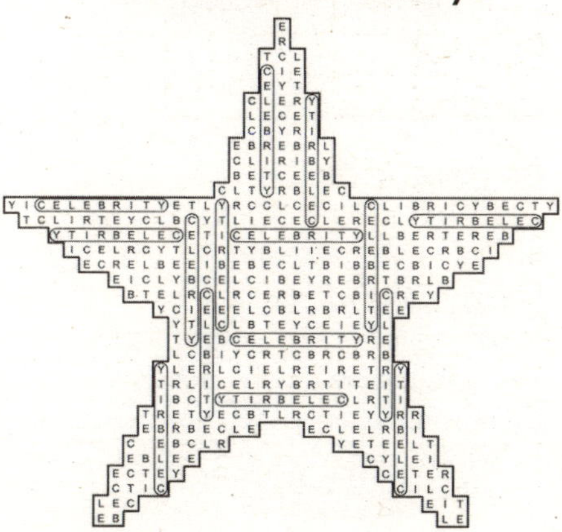

90. Mini Sudoku: Family

L	I	M	A	Y	F
F	Y	A	M	I	L
M	F	I	Y	L	A
A	L	Y	I	F	M
I	A	L	F	M	Y
Y	M	F	L	A	I

91. Cryptogram
You floated across that floor like butter on a crumpet.

92. Name Track
Natasha Kaplinsky

93. What They Said
1a, 2c, 3b

94. Word Ladder
Here is one possible solution: rise, rile, file, fill, fall.

95. Ant-icipating *Strictly*
1) significant, 2) buoyant, 3) observant, 4) pleasant, 5) instant, 6) triumphant, 7) elegant.
The word in the shaded column is 'sublime'.

96. Star Name
Motsi Mabuse

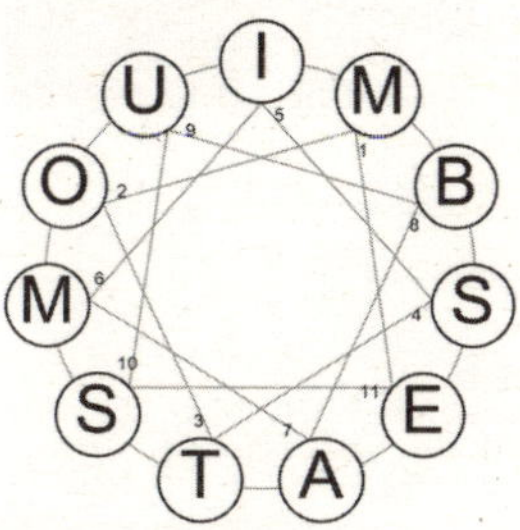

97. Letter Drop
If you think that's bad, you should see the salsa.

98. Anagrams
1) Hamza Yassin, 2) Ore Oduba, 3) Louis Smith, 4) Rose Ayling-Ellis, 5) Stacey Dooley. All of them won *Strictly*.

99. Mystery Sudoku

M	E	T	L	P	R	I	H	U
L	U	P	H	I	M	R	E	T
I	H	R	E	T	U	P	M	L
E	I	L	P	H	T	U	R	M
U	T	M	I	R	E	L	P	H
R	P	H	M	U	L	E	T	I
H	M	E	R	L	I	T	U	P
P	L	U	T	E	H	M	I	R
T	R	I	U	M	P	H	L	E

100. Take Your Pick – Craig's Paddle
1b, 2c, 3b

101. Criss-Cross

102. On Track
Dance routine.

103. Match
1c, 2g, 3i, 4f, 5d, 6a, 7j, 8b, 9h, 10e

104. A Perplexing Poser
Latin dance. Lat *in* the word dance.

105. Cryptogram
I'm looking forward to a little bit of sparkle on those dark winter nights.

106. Mini Sudoku

G	E	U	S	D	J
D	J	S	G	E	U
S	G	J	E	U	D
U	D	E	J	G	S
J	U	G	D	S	E
E	S	D	U	J	G

107. Anagrams
1) Glitterball, 2) It Takes Two, 3) Group dance, 4) Showdance, 5) Leaderboard

108. Word Search

The hidden song is 'Walking on Sunshine'.

109. A-maze-ing

110. Dominoes
1) Bill Bailey, Ellie Leach,
2) disaster, fabulous

111. Cross Out
Music

112. Follow the Leader
Nancy Xu, Vito Coppola,
Neil Jones

113. Word Builder
Celebrity

114. Strictly Word Search

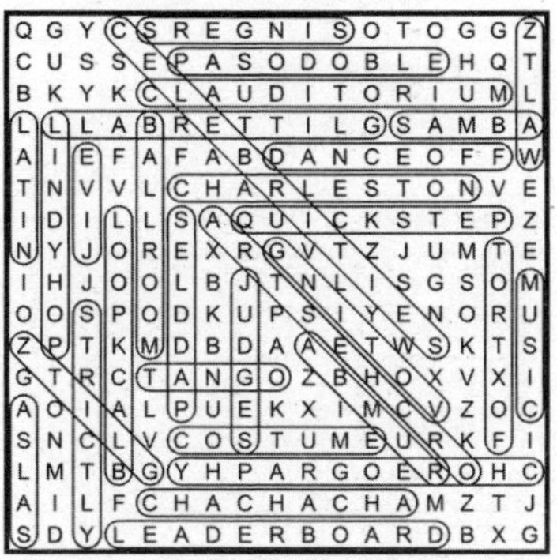

115. Crossed Words
1) Movie week, 2) Dance partner

116. Hidden Words
1) Disco, 2) Tango, 3) Chassé, 4) Latin, 5) Samba

117. Take Your Pick
1b, 2a, 3b

118. Name Track
Annabel Croft

119. Down the Middle
Live tour

120. Word Ladder
Here is one possible solution: arm, aim, aid, lid, led, leg

121. Star Name
Fleur East

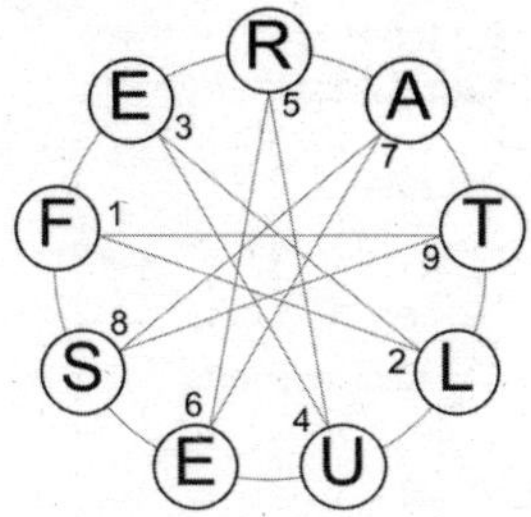

122. Cryptogram
She is absolutely over the moon having me because she really wants November off.

123. Criss-Cross

124. Letter Drop
It's incredibly compelling and heart-warming to watch people try.

125. Mini Sudoku

L	T	E	S	R	U
U	R	S	T	L	E
T	L	R	U	E	S
E	S	U	L	T	R
R	U	L	E	S	T
S	E	T	R	U	L

126. Anagrams
1) Neil Jones, 2) Amy Dowden, 3) Karen Hauer, 4) Vito Coppola, 5) Katya Jones

127. On Track
Training room

128. Word Search

O	S	L	Z	A	J	L	A
I	T	N	A	O	K	B	K
Y	K	I	W	U	U	A	D
M	A	I	V	L	R	N	I
A	T	G	E	E	R	E	A
A	Y	C	N	A	N	I	N
C	A	R	L	O	S	L	N
S	A	T	I	K	I	N	E

The other contributors are 'singers'.

129. A Perplexing Poser
Reverse Turn

130. Cross Out
Dance.

131. Match
1f, 2e, 3j, 4g, 5b, 6d, 7i, 8c, 9h, 10a

132. Mystery Word
The words need to be inserted in the following order: timing, swivel, glitzy, energy, circle and dances. The word in the shaded squares is 'twirls'.

133. What Motsi Said
1b, 2c, 3c

134. A Riddle
Stars

135. Word Ladder
Here is one possible solution: feed, seed, send, sand, band, bank, back

136. Celebrity Mix
Tasha Ghouri, Jamie Borthwick, Shayne Ward, Angela Scanlon, Alexandra Burke

137. Crossed Words
1) Heel lift, 2) Argentine Tango

138. Mystery Sudoku

O	R	I	U	Y	T	J	N	E
E	U	N	J	O	I	T	Y	R
T	Y	J	N	E	R	I	U	O
J	O	U	R	N	E	Y	I	T
R	E	T	I	J	Y	U	O	N
N	I	Y	T	U	O	R	E	J
U	J	E	Y	T	N	O	R	I
Y	N	R	O	I	J	E	T	U
I	T	O	E	R	U	N	J	Y

139. Mystery Stars
1) Tasha Ghouri, 2) Shayne Ward, 3) Ellie Leach, 4) Pete Wicks, 5) Sarah Hadland, 6) Hamza Yassin

140. Take Your Pick
1a, 2c, 3b

141. Word Search

C	N	O	E	V	A	E	W	E
U	A	G	N	R	U	T	W	F
C	L	O	N	I	P	S	G	L
A	F	F	R	Y	T	E	A	E
R	U	A	O	V	F	S	N	C
A	H	T	N	O	I	S	C	K
C	C	O	D	L	L	A	H	E
H	N	B	E	T	O	H	O	R
A	E	R	K	A	E	C	R	L

New Yorker is a step found in the Cha-cha-cha and the Rumba.

142. On the Right Track
Biodegradable glitter

143. Star Name
Ellie Leach

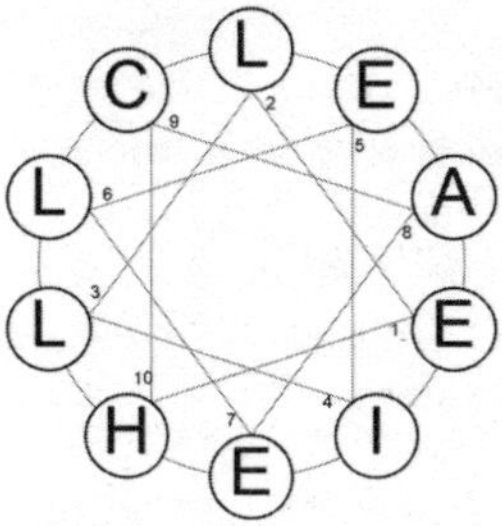

144. Crossword: On First Name Terms
ACROSS: 2) Chris, 4) Jody, 6) Aston, 9) Alex, 10) Jan, 12) Mark, 13) Angela, 14) Scott, 16) Toyah, 17) Abbey, 20) Peter, 22) Debbie, 23) Ali, 24) Helen.
DOWN: 1) Jay, 2) Clara, 3) Joe, 4) Judy, 5) Darren, 7) Ore, 8) Harry, 10) Jeremy, 11) Natasha, 12) Matt, 15) Ellie, 18) Brian, 19) Eddie, 20) Paul, 21) Rose.

145. Criss-Cross

146. Cryptogram
Passion, dedication and the ability to connect with the audience.

147. Dominoes
1) Glitterball, Leaderboard,
2) Staircase, Musicians

148. A-maze-ing

149. Props Word Search

P	S	R	P	R	P	O	S	P	S	R
O	P	R	O	O	R	P	S	P	O	R
S	S	O	P	O	P	S	O	P	O	P
P	S	R	R	O	P	S	O	P	S	R
O	S	R	P	R	R	S	R	O	P	O
S	P	O	R	O	S	O	P	P	S	S
S	R	R	S	O	P	S	R	O	P	O
S	P	R	R	S	O	R	P	R	S	P
S	R	P	O	P	O	S	P	S	R	P
O	P	R	R	P	O	R	S	O	S	O
R	O	S	R	O	P	S	O	P	R	S

150. Cross Out
Rumba

151. Trivia
1) Elephant, 2) Harry Judd,
3) Mary Poppins, 4) 2021,
5) Angela Rippon, 6) Penguin,
7) Tommy Blaize

152. Word Link
1) Left, 2) Play, 3) Cake,
4) Keep, 5) Late, 6) Near,
7) Band.
The words in the shaded column are 'Fake tan'.

153. Letter Drop
'I could not find a single thing wrong with it.' This particular dance scored a perfect 40.

154. Word Search

R	V	Y	H	P	O	R	T	P
S	O	U	L	M	R	U	E	G
E	T	U	A	U	N	M	Y	L
Z	E	R	T	S	T	B	T	I
D	T	E	I	I	R	A	R	T
A	E	L	N	C	N	T	A	Z
N	V	A	A	G	T	E	P	I
C	I	N	O	W	M	L	E	N
E	J	U	D	G	E	S	Y	T

Angela Rippon said, 'Strictly Come Dancing *is, on every level, pure entertainment,*' with the words 'pure entertainment' appearing in the word search.

155. Mystery Sudoku

N	D	I	E	H	A	T	L	O
O	A	E	L	T	I	H	N	D
T	H	L	N	O	D	I	A	E
A	N	H	O	E	L	D	I	T
L	E	T	I	D	H	A	O	N
I	O	D	A	N	T	E	H	L
D	T	O	H	A	N	L	E	I
E	L	A	T	I	O	N	D	H
H	I	N	D	L	E	O	T	A

156. Take Your Pick
1c – Sarah was also keen to teach her dance partner Vito Coppola 'full brewing etiquette', 2c, 3b

157. Fitting Words
The words need to be entered in the following order: twist, lifts, partner, music, *Strictly*, dancer, disaster and movement. The word in the shaded squares is 'staccato'.

158. Crossed Words
1) American smooth,
2) Training room

159. Celebrity Mix
Louise Redknapp, Zara McDermott, Gemma Atkinson, Bobby Brazier, Helen Skelton

160. Word Ladder
Here is one possible solution: foot, soot, shot, shop, stop, step

161. Star Name
Janette Manrara

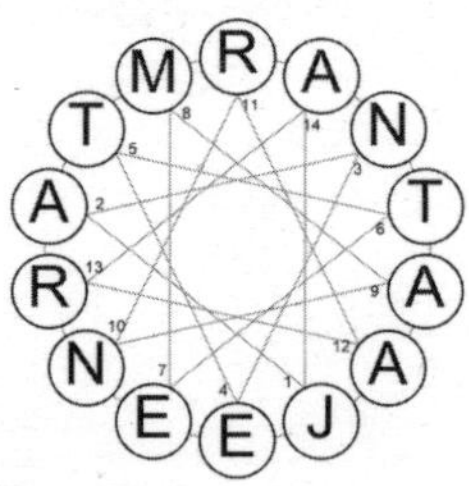

162. Mini Sudoku

E	D	A	C	N	S
N	S	C	E	D	A
A	C	D	S	E	N
S	E	N	D	A	C
C	N	E	A	S	D
D	A	S	N	C	E

163. Word Circles

1) Training, 2) audience, 3) fabulous, 4) practice, 5) applause, 6) Strictly

164. What They Said

1b, 2c, 3c

165. Follow the Leader

Tess Daly, Dave Arch, Hamza Yassin

166. Glitterball Word Search

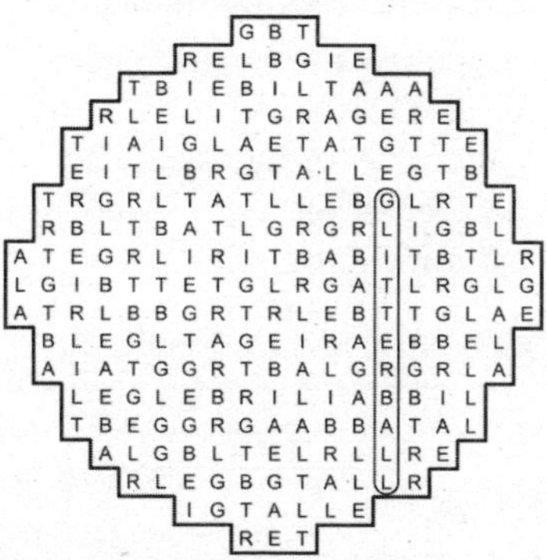

167. Dancing Target

Possible words include: acid, acing, agin, aid, and, ani, can, caning, cig, dag, dan, dig, din, ding, gad, gain, gin, inn, nag, nan, nicad

168. Christmas Word Search

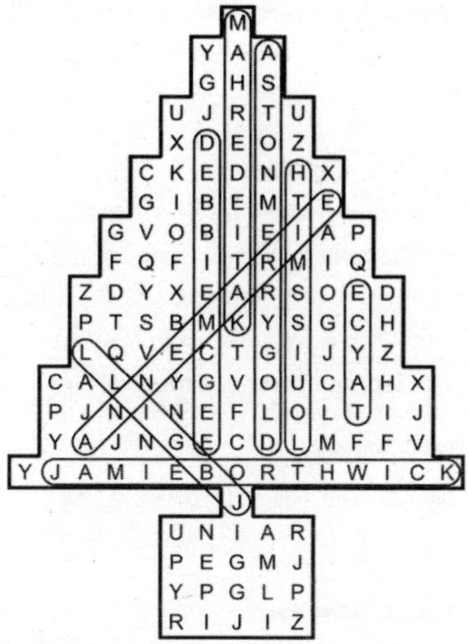

169. Mystery Sudoku

V	E	R	D	I	C	T	N	A
D	I	T	N	A	V	C	R	E
C	N	A	E	R	T	I	V	D
E	R	C	A	N	I	D	T	V
A	V	N	T	C	D	R	E	I
I	T	D	V	E	R	A	C	N
R	C	V	I	D	E	N	A	T
N	D	E	R	T	A	V	I	C
T	A	I	C	V	N	E	D	R

170. A Perplexing Poser

Elstree Studios (L's tree stew D O's)

171. Word Ladder

Here is one possible answer: warm, ward, word, wood, food, fool, cool

172. Trivia

1) The dance-off, 2) Charleston, 3) 'Keep dancing!', 4) Rumba, 5) 90 seconds, 6) Foxtrot, 7) Icons

173. Cryptogram
I have fallen in love with dance and the joy it brings to people's faces.

174. Fitting Words
The words need to be inserted in the following order: samba, heel, tango, rumba, smooth, spin, lifts, routine, waltz. The word in the shaded squares is 'beautiful'.

175. Match
1h, 2j, 3a, 4i, 5f, 6b, 7d, 8c, 9e, 10g

176. Codeword

	R		C		I		J		U		E		P	
R	E	M	A	I	N		A	P	P	E	N	D	I	X
	V		V		K		V		D		C		C	
J	A	M	E	S	B	Y	E		A	C	H	I	N	G
	L		R		L		L		T		U		I	
Q	U	A	N	G	O		I	N	E	F	F	E	C	T
	E				T		N				L			
A	D	D	R	E	S	S		E	D	B	A	L	L	S
			E				C		O				E	
T	E	S	S	D	A	L	Y		W	O	M	B	A	T
	X		E		B		P		N		I		F	
E	C	L	A	I	R		R	E	S	E	M	B	L	E
	I		T		U		E		I		I		E	
A	T	T	E	M	P	T	S		Z	E	N	I	T	H
	E		D		T		S		E		G		S	

The special nickname was 'Queen of Latin', earned by Head Judge Shirley Ballas.

177. A Riddle
Smiles

178. Mini Sudoku

T	R	F	O	A	M
M	O	A	T	R	F
R	F	T	A	M	O
A	M	O	F	T	R
O	A	R	M	F	T
F	T	M	R	O	A

179. Letter Drop
It can be done and age is no barrier to learning a new skill.

180. Crossed Words
a) Dance steps, b) American spin

181. Word Builder
Technique

182. Cross Out
Frame

183. Word Ladder
Here is one possible solution: good, gold, hold, hole, home, tome, time

184. Mystery Word
The words need to be inserted in the following order: salsa, gancho, chaîné, musicality, samba, New Yorker. The word in the shaded squares is 'shimmy'. This is a little shake of the upper body achieved by alternating shoulder movements forward and backward.

185. Word Search: The P's

P	D	H	S	V	P	M	Q	P	A	Z	Q	I
H	R	O	P	R	I	N	C	I	P	L	E	S
D	T	A	R	P	K	D	I	E	P	F	E	P
Z	P	B	C	Y	R	I	L	P	L	D	X	H
L	A	R	U	T	S	O	P	Q	E	P	Z	Y
R	T	T	C	Y	I	X	E	R	L	I	P	S
H	P	P	I	E	N	C	I	P	L	P	S	I
E	C	N	A	R	E	V	E	S	R	E	P	C
P	N	O	L	P	C	E	P	R	E	P	U	A
T	H	P	Z	E	E	F	X	I	L	U	P	L
G	L	N	O	I	T	C	E	F	R	E	P	K
I	P	R	P	E	K	H	P	N	F	O	I	I
P	E	G	N	I	S	I	M	O	R	P	R	P

186. Match
1f, 2h, 3a, 4g, 5b, 6c, 7e, 8d

187. Star Name
Shirley Ballas

188. A Strictly Conundrum
There were no letter 'e's in the paragraph. Not always 'eeee'asy to spot!

189. Between the Lines
Showdance, the dance routine performed by the top couples in the series Grand Final.

190. Hidden Names
1) Kai, 2) Gorka, 3) Karen, 4) Dianne, 5) Neil

191. Mini Sudoku

H	Y	O	T	P	R
T	R	P	H	O	Y
Y	H	R	O	T	P
P	O	T	Y	R	H
R	T	H	P	Y	O
O	P	Y	R	H	T

192. Anagrams
1) Michelle Tsiakkas,
2) Johannes Radebe, 3) Jowita Przystał, 4) Kai Widdrington,
5) Brendan Cole

193. Fitting Words
The words need to be inserted in the following order from top to bottom: costume, chassé, samba, music, tempo, Latin, ballroom, fake tan. The word created in the shaded squares, and what celebrities hope to become, is 'champion'.

194. Mystery Sudoku

M	A	I	E	T	V	R	Y	L
E	R	L	Y	I	A	M	V	T
V	T	Y	L	M	R	I	A	E
T	Y	M	V	L	I	A	E	R
A	I	R	M	Y	E	T	L	V
L	V	E	R	A	T	Y	M	I
I	L	A	T	E	Y	V	R	M
R	M	T	A	V	L	E	I	Y
Y	E	V	I	R	M	L	T	A

195. Name Track
Stacey Dooley, winner of the 2018 series of *Strictly*.

196. Letter Drop
I gave that my all and it was amazing.

197. Cross Out
Flair

198. Word Track
Clauditorium

199. A Perplexing Poser
Makeup (the word 'make' going up)

200. Cryptogram
The show is over,
sparkling memories remain.
Echoes of laughter.

ABOUT THE AUTHOR

Neil Somerville is the first to admit he cannot dance (or sing for that matter) but, like so many, is in awe of the celebrities who nobly rise to the challenge of learning to dance each year and share their experience. It shows that when you try, so much becomes possible.

When not watching *Strictly*, Neil is busy writing and compiling puzzles and has many best-selling books to his credit, including *The Train Lover's Puzzle Book*, *Cat Wisdom: 60 Great Lessons You Can Learn from a Cat* and a long-running series on Chinese horoscopes. He has also written a novel, *Legacy*.

Neil also enjoys walking, cycling, travelling, composing haiku, and is a member of the Magic Circle.

He lives in Berkshire with his wife and has two adult children.

Neil's website is www.neilsomerville.com